T0043461

JANET MELROSE &
SHERYL NORMANDEAU

*The Prairie Gardener's
Go-To for*

Trees &
Shrubs

TOUCHWOOD

TouchWood Editions
touchwoodeditions.com

The information in this book is true and complete to the best of the authors' knowledge. All recommendations are made without guarantee on the part of the authors or the publisher.

Copy edited by Paula Marchese

Designed by Tree Abraham

Photos by Janet Melrose and Sheryl Normandeau with the following exceptions:
p. 23 (Radovan1 / Shutterstock.com), p. 93 (Photo Fun / Shutterstock.com), p. 96 (Fotokostik / Shutterstock.com), p. 104 (courtesy of Gail Kozun Bruckner), p. 105 (courtesy of Tina Boisvert).

CATALOGUING DATA AVAILABLE FROM LIBRARY AND ARCHIVES CANADA

ISBN 9781771513685 (print)

ISBN 9781771513692 (electronic)

TouchWood Editions acknowledges that the land on which we live and work is within the traditional territories of the Lkwungen (Esquimalt and Songhees), Malahat, Pacheedaht, Scia'new, T'sou-ke, W̱SÁNEĆ (Pauquachin, Tsartlip, Tsawout, Tseycum) peoples.

We acknowledge the financial support of the Government of Canada through the Canada Book Fund, and the province of British Columbia through the Book Publishing Tax Credit.

This book was produced using FSC®-certified, acid-free papers, processed chlorine free, and printed with soya-based inks.

Printed in China

26 25 24 23 22 1 2 3 4 5

Dedicated to all prairie gardeners

Introduction

Imagine a world without trees and shrubs. What if the plant kingdom had evolved to include only grasses, annual plants, and forbs (otherwise known as herbaceous perennials)? What if there were no majestic trees or tangled shrubs in the understorey of our forests, woodlands, and thickets? What a loss that would be to the Earth's ecology. Trees and shrubs are the bulk of the Earth's biomass. They are responsible for carbon dioxide storage, oxygen production, movement of water, recycling of nutrients, and a host of other functions. The cycle of life of plants — especially trees and shrubs — is what makes our biosphere tick, and their importance to the health of the Earth's ecology cannot be overstated. Collectively, they contribute immensely to human survival — providing shelter, food, clothing, medicines, communication, transportation, and more. In our gardens, trees and shrubs provide numerous benefits, including reducing air, light, and noise pollution, and protecting our homes from wind, cold, and heat. Economically, they can reduce heating and air-conditioning bills. They provide habitat for life, from birds to insects and not a few squirrels, and places for children to climb and swing from.[1] We undervalue trees and shrubs at our peril!

Trees and shrubs are woody plants, as opposed to annuals or forbs. Rather than completing their life cycle in one year, like annual plants, or having their upper growth die back to the crown at the onset of winter each year as forbs do, they are permanent in the landscape with roots, stems or trunks, and branches and twigs all remaining alive throughout the four seasons. Supremely adapted to the various biomes they have evolved in, they can withstand the extremes of cold in the winter and heat and drought in the summer. With each seasonal cycle, they renew their growth, increasing in mass and stature, until they reach the end of their natural lifespans.

In *The Prairie Gardener's Go-To for Trees and Shrubs*, we offer advice and recommendations to help you successfully grow trees and shrubs from the ground up. We provide suggestions to help you choose which trees and shrubs fit your landscape in every way — from siting to sizing — and how to give them their best chance for growing at planting time. We talk about what to do once you've planted, covering best care practices for watering, fertilizing, mulching, staking, and pruning. We troubleshoot from all angles, addressing everything from girdling roots and weather-related issues to common pests and diseases. Our goal is to encourage everyone to view trees and shrubs as part of the family.[2]

—SHERYL NORMANDEAU & JANET MELROSE

One of the best reasons to grow trees and shrubs is for their beauty. These crabapple blossoms are a delight in spring!

Shrubs, like this forsythia, are multi-stemmed from ground level.

Trees are usually larger than shrubs and have a main stem called a trunk. This mountain ash will grow to between 25 and 30 feet (7.6 to 9 metres).

The science of woody plants

Plants are vascular. They have tissues called phloem and xylem that connect all parts of the plant, transporting water, nutrients, and minerals and providing structural support. Woody plants are differentiated by their ability to develop secondary woody tissue, which enables their trunks and limbs to grow in girth and length. Very simply, meristematic tissue, being undifferentiated cells capable of dividing, is found just inside bark in a layer called the vascular cambium, and is responsible for forming the secondary phloem or outer cambium toward the outside and the inner xylem or sapwood toward the inside of the plant. As with all vascular plants, the xylem is responsible for transporting water up the plant and outwards to the limbs. The phloem transports nutrients in the form of carbohydrates, down from the foliage to the roots and out to the rest of the plant. Over time the sapwood ages and dies and becomes part of the heartwood, which has the main function of supporting the plant, though it also can be a reservoir of water for the sapwood. Likewise, over time, the phloem cells age and collapse and are pushed outwards to become part of the outer bark, which protects the vulnerable cambium beneath it. This is a truly sophisticated and elegant set of adaptations that permits our woody plants to be a permanent part of our gardens![3]**—JM**

Planting and Transplanting

1

How do you determine what size of tree or shrub is appropriate for your garden?

It is easy to overplant any garden, big or little. We look at the container with that cute sapling or small shrub, and it is hard to imagine how it will look in our gardens down the road.

The key is to learn how large it will be at maturity. Consider both the height and width and take into account your growing conditions. Many common species we plant are shorter and narrower at maturity given our latitude and other factors.

Factor into the equation the distances roots grow out from the trunk or stems, using a rough guide of double the size of the height of the plant. Bear in mind barriers such as overhead power lines, property lines, and walls of houses, as you need to consider the canopy growing into neighbouring properties or sidewalks, roads, and alleys, or mashing up against the side of your own house.

This spruce tree has clearly outgrown its space. Always consider the mature size of your tree or shrub when you choose which plants to use in your landscape.

Be especially careful when deciding what types of trees to grow near power lines. This crabapple has grown dangerously close to the utility lines and now needs a drastic pruning.

Then measure out your garden and plot out the species you want to include. You will quickly see what size of trees or shrubs will match the size of your garden. Don't be tempted to choose larger species or cultivars, thinking you can prune them to the size you desire. The constant pruning will result in less healthy plants and, potentially, a shorter lifespan. Though we have all done this at least once and learned this lesson the hard way!

Larger gardens can easily accommodate standard-sized species, but smaller ones might require cultivars grown specifically for smaller gardens. Thankfully, both columnar-shaped cultivars and smaller-stature ones are readily available.[1] —JM

Ohio buckeye can top out at forty feet (twelve metres).
This one is displaying spectacular fall foliage.

What is caliper?

Caliper is a measurement of the diameter of a tree, taken at a very specific location: usually six inches (fifteen centimetres) above the root flare (the collar where the trunk naturally widens as it meets the roots). If a tree has a caliper of over four inches (one hundred millimetres), the measurement is taken twelve inches (thirty centimetres) above the root flare. In Canada, caliper is always measured in millimetres, using a manual or electronic tool also called a caliper. The Canadian Nursery Stock Standard ensures that caliper measurements are consistent and conform to minimum specifications to assist tree growers, distributors, and purchasers in obtaining standardized products.

The larger diameter of "caliper trees" (over two inches or fifty millimetres) is generally an indicator that the tree is more advanced in age and possesses a wider canopy and greater height than a sapling of the same species. The rate of growth and the growth habit for each particular tree species will affect how quickly the tree reaches a large caliper (or *if* it will!). It is likely that a fast-growing tree specimen and a slow-growing tree specimen of the same age may not have the same caliper.[2] —SN

What on earth is DBH?

You may hear the term "diameter at breast height" (DBH) in conjunction with caliper, but the two measurements are not the same. DBH is taken 4.5 feet (1.4 metres) above the root flare to measure the diameter of the trunk of a mature tree.[3] —SN

Is it best to buy big trees or shrubs or smaller ones? Why?

There are pros and cons for purchasing large plants or going with smaller ones, and one size does *not* fit all circumstances.

In a nutshell, larger plants, such as trees or shrubs, are more expensive but provide instant impact and may increase your property value. You are literally importing an almost fully grown specimen into your garden. The downsides are they are harder to plant, there will likely be delivery fees, and you may need to hire someone (possibly with machines such as a tree spade and a backhoe) to help you plant it. For success when planting a large caliper tree, it's important to dig a hole that can accommodate such a large root ball, and do not prune those roots when you plant. Ensure you have the root flare at soil level, so you don't suffocate the plant by burying it with extra soil or too-deep mulch.

Once planted, large trees require a lot of care to ensure that they do not suffer transplant shock. Their roots are much smaller than they should be for the above-ground structures, either because they have been root pruned or because they have been grown in a small container. It can take years for root systems to properly develop, and, during that time, you may not see much in the way of growth in the girth of the trunk or branches, or, indeed, in the overall size of the plant. Do not worry: as long as it appears healthy, it will all work out in time. While you're waiting, don't forget to maintain a regular watering schedule.

Smaller specimens are less expensive, primarily because the tree grower hasn't had to care for them as long. There is also a better selection of species and varieties, and they are much easier to plant yourself. Usually, smaller plants suffer less transplant shock as their root systems aren't disturbed greatly during the planting process, nor are the roots significantly smaller than the upper structures. As a result, they will resume growing almost immediately. The downside is that they can look puny for quite a while, and they are more subject to damage, given their smaller stature. We can literally forget that they are there and run them over!

However, smaller trees and shrubs will almost always catch up to the size of larger trees within three to five years because they have so much less work to do in growing roots to match their existing size. Smaller plants almost always develop better root systems since they haven't been so damaged in the first place, nor is there as much chance for the roots to girdle the plant.

So, if you have the time, the consensus is that smaller is better for both the plant's health and our ultimate satisfaction with growing a beautiful and healthy tree or shrub. It may be worth it to you to purchase a larger tree; however, it depends on the project you're undertaking, your budget, and your needs for your landscape.[4] —JM & SN

When you head to the garden centre, it's up to you to decide what size tree or shrub to purchase for your garden, but always remember to match your plants to your site! This beautiful Viburnum shrub, suitable for a smaller garden, is showing off its autumn colours.

What is a multi-grafted fruit tree? What are the pros and cons of having one?

A multi-grafted (sometimes called a combination) fruit tree is, as the name implies, multiple scions (young twigs or shoots) grafted onto a single rootstock. The species of the scions must be compatible with each other and the rootstock for the tree to survive. On the prairies, apples and crabapples (*Malus* spp.) are commonly used as scions on a multi-grafted tree. (You may have heard of — or purchased for indoor growing — citrus trees that have been multi-grafted; there are also the so-called fruit salad trees that are grown in warmer climates. These may include grafts of peaches, nectarines, plums, and apricots on the same rootstock.)

Multi-grafted fruit trees are ideal for small-space gardens, and they can be helpful in situations where you need more than one variety for cross-pollination but don't want to plant several trees. You'll have the benefit of more than one variety of fruit to choose from when it comes to harvest time — perhaps you want a cooking apple and an eating apple on the same tree or an early-producing apple and a late one.

There are a few things to consider when purchasing (or creating) a multi-grafted tree. Both the scions and the rootstock must be hardy to your region. They must all be compatible. The graft must be properly performed and the site of the graft (the union) needs to be clean and healthy. You may also have to take on some extra pruning tasks in the early stages of the tree's growth, as occasionally one variety will be dominant over another and may need a little heading back to achieve balance.[5] —SN

I've just received a bare-root tree from a nursery. How do I prepare it for planting?

Bare-root plants are just that: plants that have been grown in soil, then are dug up in the fall when dormant. The surrounding soil is removed, the plants are stored during the winter to maintain dormancy, and then they are sold as is in the early spring. Bare-root plants are a cheaper option, and advocates cite the ease of handling and planting, plus the ability to order online for a greater selection than what might be available locally. Transplant shock is not as much of an issue if bare-root trees are planted as soon as you get them since they are still in dormancy.

Bare-root stock arrives from the nursery with its roots packed in damp medium such as sawdust, coir, or peat moss. The plant is usually wrapped in plastic. The key to success with a bare-root plant is to ensure that the roots don't dry out. Don't store the plant for any length of time—get it into the ground as soon as possible. To that end, carefully note the shipping date of any bare-root stock you order to be certain that the timing will be right for you to plant. The night before you want to plant bare-root stock, pull it out of the plastic, and gently brush away all of the medium from the roots. You can compost the medium, or use it as a soil amendment or mulch. Grab a large bucket and fill it with water. Dunk the plant, roots down, into the bucket, and leave it there to soak until morning.

You're going to dig a slightly unusual hole for bare-root stock. You want a hole that is wide enough to accommodate the root system of the plant when it is fully spread out, but you also want to take some of the backfill soil and create a mound in the very centre of the hole. Set the centre of the tree roots at the proper planting depth on top of this mound and carefully drape the roots out to their full length into the rest of the hole. The mound makes it easier for the roots to completely extend. Backfill the hole.

Some bare-root stock, such as hawthorn, hackberry, and European mountain ash, benefit from a process called "sweating." This helps them break dormancy and spurs budding and leafing out. To sweat a plant, you need to find a location that can be kept moist and warm—such as the inside of a heated shed or greenhouse. The temperature should be between 45 and 70°F (7 and 21°C). Lay the bare-root plant on its side and cover with damp straw. Cover the plant with a plastic sheet or tarp. Let the plant sit until the buds break. This usually takes up to a week, but it will happen faster if the room you are keeping the plant in is on the higher end of the temperature range. Every day or two, check the tree to ensure it is still damp. Add water, if needed. Once the tree is sweated, it must be planted right away.

One final thing: conifers should not be sweated. Most deciduous trees don't really need it either, but for those that have trouble breaking cold dormancy, it can be helpful.[6]—SN & JM

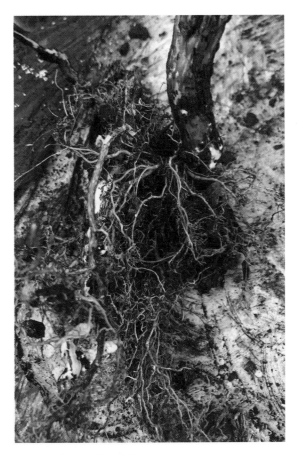

Bare-root plants need special care to prepare them for planting.

How do I deal with a ball-and-burlapped tree? Do I have to take the burlap and the wire off before planting?

Ball-and-burlapped (B&B) trees are generally large caliper, field-grown trees sold with the root ball encased in soil and bundled in burlap. They are dug up the year they are sold. The goal is to preserve as much of the root system as is feasible, but in the process of digging, there is often considerable damage and many roots may be severed, particularly the smaller, newest ones that do much of the work in taking up moisture and nutrients. Really large trees will often have a wire cage around them for support during transport. If there is a wire cage, carefully snip it away from the root ball with a pair of wire cutters.

Although burlap that is made of natural fibres, such as jute, will slowly decompose in the ground, some burlap is made of polyester. One way to tell them apart is by the way they smell, as jute has a rich, earthy scent, but it's difficult to do an accurate test of this while the fabric is on the tree (and sniffing tree roots is admittedly a bit weird!). It's best to err on the side of caution and remove the burlap before planting. This is usually a bit tricky and onerous, and you'll probably need a pair of scissors to cut it off. Place the tree in the planting hole and have a helper tilt it to one side while you work on removing the burlap. Go slow and be gentle during this task; try not to break any of the tree roots.

B&B plants are expensive, as you are buying a much larger plant. They are also heavy and may require delivery in a special truck and the use of a Bobcat to plant. They may be subject to transplant shock without proper care and, due to the amount of root loss, may be slow to re-establish. The benefit is they can be planted at any time during the growing season. They also provide the opportunity to have a larger specimen in the garden if instant impact is desired.[7] —SN & JM

Carefully remove the burlap from the root ball of a B&B tree.

Is there anything I can do if the roots of my recently purchased container tree look pot-bound?

Container plants are grown in pots, usually filled with a lighter growing medium than garden soil. The plants are grown until they have established root systems. The benefits are the ability to purchase and plant them at any point in the growing season and the relative ease of planting and establishing them in their new home. They are more expensive than bare-root plants, as the cost includes the care at a nursery over one or more seasons.

If possible, arrest the potential for purchasing root-bound nursery stock before you haul out your credit card. If the plants are root-bound, they have been in the container too long. We realize it can be tricky to lift a very heavy tree out of its pot to take a look, but check to see if there are any roots growing out of the holes in the bottom of the container. If there are any, chances are it is root-bound. Because of the confines of the container, it is normal to find a few encircling roots—you just don't want to see a tightly wound mass of trouble, especially if there are large roots growing inward. If left unchecked, this will certainly lead to girdling of the tree. If there are a few circling roots, use your gloved hands to loosen them—or for tighter clusters, use a pair of pruners to gently slice them apart so you can separate them. Don't make too many cuts or you'll damage the plant. Transplant shock can be an issue if the roots are disturbed greatly.—SN & JM

How do I dig a suitable hole for my new tree or shrub?

Planting your tree or shrub correctly will make the difference to its health and ultimate survival. Our instinct to make holes too deep is often cited as the number one reason for the premature death of our plants.[8] The reason is that the roots of plants will suffocate if there ends up being significantly more soil on top of them than where they were before being planted in your garden.

Going the other direction and making the hole the same size as the container the plant comes in is just as bad, as the roots will just sit there in the hole while they figure out what to do. I have been guilty of doing just that one year when I was in a rush. But at least the plants in question were not buried too deep, and even though it took forever for the roots to penetrate the sides of the holes and start growing, eventually the plants established themselves, and they are now thriving. Not the way to give your plants their best start!

Before you dig, take the plant out of its wrapping or container a day or so before it is to be planted and give it a huge drink so it is well-hydrated before being transplanted. At the same time, examine the base of the plant to see if it was planted too deeply to begin with. (This is particularly important for container-grown plants.) What you are looking for is the flare at the base of the trunk of

A spacious planting hole is tops for a healthy root system.

your tree or the base of the crown if it is a shrub. This is where lateral woody roots originate and where the plant should be level with the surface of the soil once it is planted in the ground.

Dig a hole no deeper than the depth of the roots up to the flare or crown and at least two to three times wider. Instead of a semicircle shape, the hole should be flat on the bottom with the sides angling outwards. Then rough up the floor and sides of the hole so that the roots will easily penetrate the soil. This step is essential if your soil is heavy clay, as the sharp metal of shovels creates smooth and largely impenetrable surfaces. Save the soil being removed on a tarp so it is close at hand. Now you are ready to go ahead with the planting![9]—JM

Stay safe!

Before planting a tree or shrub, consider . . .

*   Checking your Real Property Report (RPR) for easements. Any tree or shrub planted in these areas is automatically the property of the municipality. They cannot be pruned, treated, or removed without approval from that entity. They also can be dug up without ceremony by the municipality for any reason, including utility or roadwork.
*   Getting utility lines checked out. You don't want to dig and penetrate any buried lines! Most provinces have free services for this purpose.
*   Using the proper equipment. Planting trees and shrubs properly requires exertion and can be injurious to you. Back braces and tools with the correct handle length mean you won't need to go to physio afterward!—JM

Hawthorns, which produce fragrant white
or light pink flowers in the spring and red
"haws" in the autumn, are commonly used as
plantings in prairie municipalities.

When planting a tree or shrub, do I backfill the hole with new soil or should I use the soil I dug out?

It is by far better to use the soil you removed from the planting hole as backfill. It may seem like a great time to improve the soil that will surround the new plant after digging the hole, but woody plants, like the rest us, will take the path of least resistance and grow roots where it is easiest to do so. The result is roots growing only to the edge of the planting hole and then circling around, with all the potential problems that creates.

Different sources will say it is okay to add varying amounts of new soil and/or organic matter to improve the soil—many gardeners have traditionally sworn by throwing a handful of bone meal down the planting hole, for example—but others cite problems with the organic matter degrading under potentially anaerobic conditions.

Much better to use the soil you dug out to make the hole, layering it into the hole by thirds, watering it after each third so that large air holes are not created. Then reserve any remaining backfill to layer on once the soil has settled, or create a bit of a dam around the planting hole so water can stay close to the roots rather than draining away.

After a week or two, add a layer of compost, which will provide nutrients and work to improve the soil. Top off with an organic mulch.[10] —JM

What is a tree well? Should I make one?

In landscaping, the term "tree well" describes a large circle around the base of a tree, created to separate the tree from the surrounding turfgrass. A well can be an aesthetically pleasing way to frame the base of the tree, but, more importantly, it can protect the roots and the bark of the tree from being harmed by machines such as lawn mowers and weed trimmers by creating a barrier of distance. (Tree injuries can, in turn, lead to infestations of pests and diseases.) Bear in mind if your soil is predominantly heavy clay, a tree well isn't necessarily a good idea — in such a case, it is more important to make sure your drainage is sloping away from the plant, which may involve creating some shallow swales.

Many gardeners mulch tree wells with bark chips, which helps conserve moisture at a tree's roots and acts as a barrier to weeds. To make a tree well, create a ring of mulch about two inches (five centimetres) deep to surround the tree. The ring should extend out to the drip line. A tree well helps conserve moisture in the soil and gets it down to a tree's roots, where it is needed. This is especially important during the first year after planting while the tree is establishing itself.

If your tree well is not draining properly, it may be an indicator that your soil is predominantly clay-based. You may need to remove the well to prevent the tree from becoming oversaturated with moisture.

(After that, you can remove the well, if you wish.) If you notice the tree well is constantly full of water and is posing a drainage issue, remove it earlier—and hope that you planted a tree species that can deal with consistently damp conditions! While you can certainly ring the tree with decorative bricks or other types of edging, be sure not to hammer any of it into the ground to prevent damage to the tree's roots. As well, don't fill the well with soil—this may look lovely, but it can prevent the tree from properly taking up nutrients and water, and it can block air circulation. Rot may be a consequence.

Many gardeners love the look of the rubber mulch rings you can purchase to place around the base of your tree—and they *can* work to suppress weeds. However, they can become an issue as the tree grows, possibly trapping moisture and soil against the trunk and creating a haven for rot. In extreme cases, they may even promote girdling. Using wood chips or rocks for mulch is healthier, as long as you pull the mulch back away from the trunk of the tree. Don't push the chips or other types of mulch right up against the trunk as this can promote rot. We're serious about that notorious mulch volcano: it's never, ever a good idea!

In certain cases, you may need to create a dry tree well to protect a valuable tree when construction around it causes the grade to be raised. Changes to grade around an existing tree can cause huge problems for drainage, nutrient and water uptake, and air circulation—and it can potentially kill the tree. If the tree cannot be moved, and it is worth saving, you'll need to give it a way to cope with the grade changes. A dry tree well made from perforated pipes and washed gravel can help mitigate drainage issues.[11]—SN

When is the best time to plant or transplant trees and shrubs?

All things being equal, the best season to plant our woody species is in the early fall. The reason for that is because of their cycle of growth. Once our trees and shrubs have shed their leaves in the fall and are preparing for winter dormancy (or, in the case of evergreens, slowing their metabolism and photosynthesis), they continue to grow roots well into the early winter and only stop once the soil has completely frozen. Root growth resumes in the late winter, well before we notice them leafing out and resuming photosynthesis. In the spring and throughout the summer, most of our woody plants' energies are devoted to growing stems, leaves, flowers, and fruit, and harnessing enough energy for all of that activity.

So, by planting our trees and shrubs in the fall, we are doing so at the point in their cycle when they will be re-establishing and developing roots without having to do anything else, all in cooler conditions that reduces stress on the plants. Transplanting trees and shrubs in the spring when they are leafing out means they have to re-establish those roots at the same time they are devoting energy to their upper structures, and at a time when the season is building up to often intense summer heat. This frequently leads to premature leaf drop, due to the stress of being transplanted, plus the inability of plants to draw up enough moisture and nutrients with limited and/or disrupted root systems.

But all things are not equal on the prairies with our highly variable seasons. The window for planting once the heat of the summer is past and full freeze-up occurs can be as long as three months or as short as four to six weeks. Do we care to chance the early onset of winter, which means there wouldn't be enough time for the plants to settle in and start growing roots? Or, after reading the weather tea leaves, do we take the plunge? Or do we believe we will have an early and gentle spring with enough time for our plants to settle in nicely before the summer heat arrives?

An additional factor is whether the plants available at the end of the season will be in good condition, or will even be the species you need. On the plus side, there are usually good prices to be had as garden centres and tree farms try to move their remaining stock. In the spring, there is usually plentiful stock and a variety of plants, and everything is generally in great shape.

Regardless of whether you choose the fall or the spring for transplanting or planting trees and shrubs, critical care is needed for at least six months to a year to moderate soil temperatures and conserve moisture for any newly planted specimens' benefit.

So, the definitive answer is "It depends," and should you consult three experts, you are likely to get three or maybe four different opinions as to which is best. It really comes down to your location, particular climate, availability of plants, personal preferences, and your ability to give the plants the care they will need for each season.[12] —JM

Should I stake newly planted trees? If so, how should it be done?

If you live in an extremely windy location or you are putting in bare-root trees, we recommend staking trees when planting them. (In most other situations, it simply isn't necessary—indeed, not staking trees may help them to produce more roots and thicker, more durable trunks.)

If you are planting a small tree under six feet (1.8 metres) tall, or if the site isn't the recipient of gale-force winds on a regular basis, the two-stake method is sufficient. Pound two tall metal or wooden stakes into the ground on opposite sides of the tree. Make sure you line up the stakes so they face in the direction of the prevailing wind. (You don't want to make a mistake with this, or you really won't be helping the tree at all.) Make sure the stakes are placed just outside the root ball of the tree, not within it, as close proximity may damage the roots. Tie the tree snugly in place to the stakes using strong rope or wire, but ensure the part that goes around the trunk is made of soft material, so that it doesn't harm the bark. The tethers on the trunk should be placed approximately 4 feet (1.2 metres) off the ground. Placing them too low will accomplish very little in the way of providing stability.

If your tree will be consistently exposed to high winds, it may be a good idea to re-evaluate your planting site (or plant more trees so it doesn't face the onslaught alone!). If you really want to put the tree on a windy site, use a three-stake method to keep it tethered while it establishes its roots. The principle is the same as the two-stake method, except you're adding an extra stake for more strength. Tie it snugly, but with a bit of give so that the tree can move naturally. No matter which method you use, remove the stakes and ropes one year after planting the tree. The roots should be well-established by then, and leaving the ties in place can end up girdling the tree trunk as it grows.[13]—SN

Cultivation and Maintenance

2

How much mulch should I apply to the base of my trees?

The accepted rule of thumb is to apply two to four inches (five to ten centimetres) of mulch to cover the ground. That depth provides all the benefits of mulching without it becoming a huge task or cost. Lately, though, to encourage wildlife habitat in my garden, I have been reducing the amount of mulch I use to less than 1 inch (2.5 centimetres) deep so bees and other critters can access the soil underneath. I even leave the odd patch barely strewn for that purpose. The benefits seem to be the same with less mulch, and I have lots of bees.

The real danger is over-mulching. Gardeners always believe if something is worth doing, then more is better! Too much mulch reduces air permutation into the soil and can even suffocate roots. It damages the trunk and stems of plants by being piled up against them. Too deep a layer also is a great environment for pathogens and insect pests to take hold and for rodents to bury in and chew on the bark. That excessive layer builds up heat as it decomposes, detrimentally affecting soil temperatures.

Overenthusiastic mulching creates volcanoes of our woody plants, and I often expect to see one erupt with a tree going up in flames! Remediating a volcano is a lot of work and needs to be done slowly so the plant can adjust. No need to go there in the first place.

One final note: woody plants should be mulched out to their drip lines. The wider the area the mulch covers, the better, and you won't have to mow that part of the lawn![1] —JM

What types of mulch are best to use with trees and shrubs?

Mulching around trees and shrubs provides multiple benefits, such as conserving moisture in the soil, moderating soil temperatures, building soil texture, suppressing weeds, and reducing soil erosion. It also prevents grass from growing up around tree trunks, deters rodents from nibbling on young bark, and reduces the chance of damage from lawn mowers and whipper snippers. That makes eight wins from one simple practice!

My preference is for organic mulches that break down over time and contribute to soil texture and structure, encouraging soil life. I also reach for the ones that would naturally occur in a woodland setting. Top of my list is gardener's gold—compost. When spread on the surface, it is a wonderful mulch. A runner-up is autumn leaves, crunched up so they aren't whole, and layered on top. By midsummer they will break down and be a part of the soil, just in time for another layer in the fall. Leaf mould, from leaves gathered last year and allowed to decay for a year, is another option. Bark mulches are a super choice, too. A major plus is they take longer to degrade. Montane mulches made from pine and spruce needles mimic what is on the forest floor. Shredded mulches take longer to break down and can be their natural colour or dyed. (The dye is usually vegetable-based.) I avoid cedar, as it has natural antibacterial and antifungal properties that can affect soil life. It also takes longer to degrade, can irritate those sensitive to its smell, and is a more expensive option. Similarly, I don't use bark nuggets as they are too large to provide the best benefits for mulching. Never use fresh wood chips as they need to dry out and age. They may cause nitrogen inhibition, even on the surface of the soil. As the microbes get to work on them, they also generate a lot of heat and steam, even if you use just a thin layer. You don't want the neighbours thinking your garden is on fire!

Inorganic mulches, such as crushed rock or gravel, are also popular as they don't break down. They conserve soil moisture, but provide none of the other benefits of mulching. A disadvantage is they will absorb the sun's energy each day and will heat up the soil below the mulch, which can negatively affect the health of roots and soil life. I also find inevitably inorganic mulches end up being worked into the underlying soil and become a pain in the neck to work around. Some gardeners put down landscape fabric to avoid the rocks being mixed into the soil, which brings with it a host of other problems, such as encouraging roots to grow up into the fabric rather than down; interfering with water percolation, air exchange, and the nutrient cycle; destroying the soil microbiology; introducing a petroleum product into the soil; and becoming a maintenance issue as it inevitably degrades. I save landscape fabric and inorganic materials for pathways![2] —JM

This barberry has been mulched with wood chips.

What is the best method to water my trees and shrubs?

Newly planted and well-established mature trees and shrubs call for different watering regimes, but need the same care and attention.

Newly planted trees and shrubs often require more root mass than they possess to sustain their growth above the soil line and are not able to efficiently access surrounding soil moisture. It will take one to three seasons for their roots to establish themselves enough to support their existing superstructure, depending on how much root mass was lost through transplanting. It is essential to maintain consistent moisture in the soil surrounding these plants throughout the growing season to facilitate root establishment and to reduce the stress of moisture loss.

The first couple of weeks after planting, a tree or shrub should be watered daily, as it will only be able to uptake water in the immediate vicinity of the planting hole. Because you are watering every day, replace only what the plant will ordinarily transpire. Too much water, and one risks drowning it. A handy guideline for trees is to measure the diameter of the trunk, and for each inch (2.5 centimetres), slowly apply 1 to 1½ gallons (4 to 6 litres) of water around the planting hole. A shrub needs approximately ¼ to ⅓ the volume of the container it was grown in.

Depending on how hot or cold it has been, after the first two weeks, extend the schedule to every two or three days. Then, after three months, water the plant weekly. In the second season, increase the spread of the water beyond the planting hole as the roots will be growing a good eighteen inches (forty-five centimetres) yearly if there are ideal growing conditions. In further years, move to the regime for well-established plants (see below), assuming the tree or shrub is thriving.

Well-established trees and shrubs should be deeply watered when the soil surrounding the drip line is dry below six to nine inches (fifteen to twenty-three centimetres), which will be highly dependent on the weather, your soil composition, and whether you have applied mulch. A good trick is to dig a small hole within the drip line, six to nine inches (fifteen to twenty-three centimetres) deep, around trowel or hand size, and literally check how the soil feels inside the hole before deciding whether to water. Apply water slowly to the root zone area, which is roughly twice the height of the plant, and a bit more for good measure. There is no need to water next to the trunk or crown as the lateral roots there don't take up water. Watch the water as it sinks in. When the rate of absorption slows or you see runoff, stop and check the soil moisture in the hole. If the soil still seems dry, then wait a bit and water again, which will allow for the water to percolate the entire area. Unless it is extremely hot, the plant should be fine for a couple of weeks. Watering in this way will encourage deeper roots, which the plant will need to seek the underlying soil moisture. Refrain from light and frequent watering, which will embolden roots to grow up to the surface, where they will be vulnerable to drought stress.

The rule of thumb for watering is to water slowly and steadily, rather than pouring great splashes of water all at once, and to water deliberately, rather than casually. Your trees and shrubs will thank you for doing so![3] —JM

*This happy Viburnum shrub has been watered sufficiently
and has established itself in its planting site.*

When should I stop watering my trees and shrubs before the winter freeze-up?

It is tempting to keep watering our woody plants well into the fall, especially if we have one of those hot and dry autumns. However, doing so doesn't do them any favours, as they are about to go into dormancy to survive the winter. The process is initiated once the daylight hours dwindle and growth slows and stops. Deciduous woodies lose their leaves (a process called abscission), followed by water withdrawing from their cells, which increases the levels of sugars and creates their own form of antifreeze to protect them against the freezing weather to come. Evergreens undergo the same process, just not as obviously. Continuing to water spurs the plant to continue growing and defers the dormancy process until it's too late.

Stop providing additional water by early fall. I usually do so around Labour Day, when deciduous leaves are yellowing and evergreens are starting to drop some of their innermost needles.

But then, just before winter hits and while the soil is still unfrozen, provide one last deep watering. A good time to do this is in late October after the trees have fully lost their leaves. My mental calendar always has a note to do so the week before Hallowe'en. No matter how nice it has been beforehand, we always seem to get that first winter storm and cold snap around then![4]—JM

Give your trees and shrubs a big glug of H_2O once all the gorgeous leaves drop.

When should I fertilize an established or mature tree? What type of fertilizer should I use?

You may be surprised to hear this, but you don't have to fertilize your mature trees and shrubs very often. If your soil isn't absolutely depleted of nutrients, and your plants appear to be doing just fine, don't bother. It's one less task you need to write on your gardening to-do list. You never want to apply fertilizer when it's not necessary or overfertilize because you think more is better—the accelerated growth this can cause may actually weaken the plants in the long run and make them targets for pests and diseases. If you have done a soil test and deficiencies have been flagged, then fertilizing will be necessary. In many cases, a side-dressing of 1 to 2 inches (2.5 to 5 centimetres) of compost will be enough. This may be applied once a year, in the spring, until the issue has corrected itself.[5] —SN

Keep weeds and turfgrass from encroaching on your trees and shrubs!

Keeping the vicinity of your trees and shrubs free of grass and weeds will allow your trees to freely take up nutrients and water without having to share. This is particularly important for newly planted trees, which need all the competitive edge they can get (in terms of water, nutrients, and rooting space) to establish themselves. And if you're growing fruit trees or shrubs, competition from other plants in the area may actually cause issues with fruit production.

I recommend applying a four-inch (ten-centimetre) layer of organic mulch, such as straw or wood chips, at the base of the tree or shrub to create a barrier to weeds and turfgrass. (Do not use landscape fabric beneath the mulch—it will cause more problems than it's worth.) If you notice a few stray plants are creeping into the mulch, manually remove them by pulling them out.—**SN**

What does it mean to "top" a tree? Is this ever a good idea?

When a tree is topped, terminal (end) shoots are removed. This means the entire top of the tree is cut off, leaving stubby, lateral branches and no suitable material to replace the severed leader. Gardeners sometimes think they need to perform this drastic procedure when their trees have grown too close to power lines or are casting too much shade due to their large size, or if they have been damaged in a storm, but topping trees is almost never warranted (unless, of course, you are practising some of the more extreme, deliberate methods of pruning such as pollarding).

Not only does topping a tree severely reduce its aesthetic appeal, but it can be extremely detrimental to a tree's health, causing immense stress and increasing the potential of pest infestations. Multiple leaders will spring up over time, further damaging a tree's once good looks, and this new growth will lack the strength and structure the tree originally possessed. The weaker growth may not be able to withstand high winds or storms, and the tree may become a hazard. You definitely don't want to have to pay up if your tree breaks and falls onto your neighbour's house! To keep this growth in check, you will need to keep pruning, usually on an annual basis, which means a lot more work and expense for you.

Understanding the problems associated with tree topping should be a factor in the back of your mind when shopping for a tree. Don't purchase a tree that will outgrow your yard—even if you plan to live on the property for only a short amount of time. Don't leave an expensive legacy to the homeowners who will one day buy the property from you. If you have power lines in your yard, pay very close attention to the mature height listed on the tags of the trees and shrubs you select to plant beneath them. And if for some reason your tree needs to be radically resized, call a certified arborist to do the job. There are ways to prune and manage tree height that don't involve topping, and if things are really drastic, the tree may need to be removed. A consultation with a professional can help you make a decision about the best course of action.[6]—SN

Topped trees usually have diminished aesthetic value, and they may even weaken over time.

How much should you prune trees or shrubs?

The short answer is: it depends!

Newly planted trees and shrubs should not be pruned at all, except for damaged stems and limbs, until the roots are well-established, and they have overcome transplant shock. The plants will need all of their existing branches and stems to generate the energy they will need to settle into their new surroundings.

Once a tree or shrub is into its third year of growing and is healthy, you will want to establish a regular routine of training and pruning so that it grows into the shape you want it to be. The usual rule of thumb is to remove a third of a shrub's stems every year so the plant is constantly renewed. Choose the oldest stems and prune back to the crown. Some garden- ers use a five-year renewal cycle, rather than the more drastic three-year cycle for shrubs. There are some exceptions to this rule though. The type of plant can be a factor, with fruit-bearing trees requiring annual pruning to promote fruit buds. Deciduous trees are likely to require more pruning than evergreens, which can go for years without needing pruning unless there is damage or they develop prob- lems in their structure.

The key is to remove enough stems to promote the development of new ones by stimulating dormant buds but without upsetting the balance of the plant's root mass to upper growth ratio. Remove too little, and you will fail to stimulate new growth to any degree. Remove too much, and the plant either will respond by growing suckers and water sprouts or may decide the injury is too much and will go toes up. A word to the wise: if I am in doubt as to whether to remove that stem or branch, I wait a year.

Trees that are well-established should continue to receive regular pruning to train their framework and eliminate any untoward growth, every two or three years, depending on how fast any given tree is maturing. Trees that have reached maturity require less pruning, perhaps on a five-year cycle, with an upper limit of 10 percent removed at any one time. Extremely old trees should have even less removed at a time, perhaps 5 percent, and only if really warranted.

Once a shrub or tree reaches old age, prune only what needs to come out to maintain good health, without encour- aging further growth in size.[7] **—JM**

Should individual shrubs or hedges ever be sheared down to nearly ground level? How do you do this?

There are only a couple of reasons to hard prune a shrub back to its crown. The first is if it has become an overgrown, unruly mess, and there is no way to restore its shape without drastic measures. In such a case, it is likely its new growth is being inhibited too, as the growth buds may have become dormant.

As for hedges, hard pruning is sometimes called for due to incorrect trimming, usually in cases where the inside of the hedge is barren of any leaves, and the individual plants have lost their vigour with only the very outside stems being able to generate energy for the whole plant.

Hard pruning is extremely tough on the plant and should only be used on those species that are naturally vigorous growers and generate lots of twiggy stems. Think dogwood, spirea, and potentilla. Other candidates that have fewer stems overall but are vigorous plants can respond well to this treatment, such as forsythia, lilac, and weigela. Prairie gardeners hard prune Annabelle hydrangea (*Hydrangea arborescens* 'Annabelle') every year simply because in the winter its stems always get killed to the soil level in our climate. The hard pruning stimulates the dormant buds into action and generates new growth in a hurry.

Avoid hard pruning any shrub or hedge that has only a few main stems per plant. These are often older shrubs that may not have what it takes to rejuvenate in this manner. All you will get is the nub of the plant staring back at you, possibly with a couple of weakly growing new stems, reproaching you for your plant-icide. Instead of a hard prune, these plants should be rejuvenated over a longer period, with regular pruning of older stems. The exception to the rule is cotoneaster (*Cotoneaster* spp.) that are dying back due to being infested with oystershell scale. Hard prune out all the stems and dispose of them in the garbage, and likely the hedge will regrow nicely.

Any shrub that has been grafted should be treated with care to avoid pruning below the graft union. Evergreen shrubs should never be hard pruned!

Always perform hard pruning in late winter before the shrub leaves dormancy. You want all of the energy stored in the roots and available for new growth. Make the cuts approximately six inches (fifteen centimetres) above ground, but don't simply whack every stem willy-nilly. What you want to look for is an outward-facing node or bud and prune the stem just above it, about ¼ inch (6 millimetres), at an angle, so that the high point is just above the bud, which will promote new growth. Stems that are cut higher will have a tougher time budding out.

Once you have finished, wait for the shrub to start sending up new growth. Then fertilize carefully so the plant has lots of nutrients available, but not so much that there is an excessive amount of succulent growth at once, which can weaken the plant and attract pathogens such as powdery mildew. I prefer extra compost or worm compost for the job, perhaps with some fish meal added.

Once the plant has generated new growth, select three or four stems to promote as the main stems. Allow the plant to grow back to its true size and shape over the next few years by continuing to train it with selective pruning. Then you can easily implement a regimen to ensure the plant continues to be vigorous but well-behaved.[8] —JM

Potentillas generally respond well to hard pruning.

Should you prune evergreens? If so, when should it be done?

Conifers such as spruce, fir, and pine typically do not require pruning except to remove dead or diseased branches or to promote a denser growth habit. Casually removing entire branches will only result in gaping holes that will ruin a tree's aesthetic. But if you are looking to encourage a bushier form, annual spring pruning is actually a good idea.

For spruce and fir trees, remove all fresh new growth by up to half its length. This can typically be done in early June, but it will depend on the weather.

Pines need to be treated a bit differently because they only bud out at the tips, unlike spruce and fir (which form buds along the length of their stems). With pines, wait until you see the new "candles" at the tips of the branches, then cut off up to half of their length. This will spur new terminal buds to form wherever you have made cuts, resulting in more growth the following year.

Junipers—both ground cover and upright forms—may be trimmed in the spring to remove tips that may have been browned by dry winter winds. Performing another trim of the new growth once it has emerged will also promote a denser appearance. Again, only cut up to half of the length of the new growth.[9]—SN

Mugo pines have very obvious candles in the spring.

What is the proper timing for pruning deciduous trees and shrubs on the prairies?

Timing your pruning to match the growing cycle of your woody plants will result in healthier plants, without interrupting the flowering and fruiting cycle of flowering plants, and avoiding creating open wounds, which invite in pathogens and insects. In some instances, pruning must be undertaken within certain dates if required by law (see sidebar).

Autumn is not the best time. The injuries caused by pruning will stimulate growth, rather than allowing your woodies to slip into dormancy before winter hits. Assess what needs to be pruned, however, and mark where pruning should occur. However, if there is a storm that wreaks havoc on trees that are still fully in leaf, that damage must be dealt with promptly. "Snow-tember 2014" in Calgary left many trees in a dangerous state over that winter.

Late winter or early spring, before buds start to unfurl, is generally the kindest time as the plant will be healing itself with the growth that comes naturally at that time of year. This practice also avoids creating open wounds for unwanted guests to enter. It is especially true if you live in an area where there is an epidemic of any sort, such as black knot.

To avoid losing a year's worth of fabulous flowering, keep in mind the timing. Shrubs that bloom past the midsummer solstice set their flower buds on new wood, so there is more flexibility regarding when to prune. On the other hand, lilac, forsythia, and other early-flowering shrubs should be pruned right after they finish flowering, as they set flower buds for the next year almost immediately on current wood, which complicates things.

There are exceptions. Trees with heavy sap loads, such as birch and maple, are better pruned once they have fully leafed out, simply to avoid the sap running down the trunk and staining the bark.[10] —JM

What is the law regarding the time of year to prune elm trees?

In some parts of Canada, there are provincial laws regarding when elm (*Ulmus* spp.) trees may be pruned. Dutch elm disease (DED) is the reason for the pruning bans: a couple of types of fungus (*Ophiostoma ulmi* and *O. novo-ulmi*) spread by elm bark beetles can easily and rapidly decimate elm populations. Infected trees located close to one another can also transfer the fungal spores via root grafts.

The trees must be pruned when the beetles are not active, as the insects are attracted to the volatile oils generated by fresh pruning cuts made during the warmer months.

Pruning bans:

Alberta: April 1 to September 30

Saskatchewan: April 1 to August 31

Manitoba: April 1 to July 31

If you are pruning an infected elm tree, be sure to sterilize your cutting tools between cuts using a commercial disinfectant.

Do not transport or store infected elm wood—this isn't the stuff you should be using in your firepit!

If you decide to plant elm trees, select DED-resistant cultivars, such as 'Patriot', 'Pioneer', and 'New Horizon'. (Match up your hardiness zones to ensure they will work in your garden!)[11] **—SN**

These elm trees are just starting to sport fall foliage in early September. Observe the pruning ban on these beauties to maintain their health.

Do I have to apply any sealant to pruning cuts?

The short answer is No!

The practice of using petroleum-based paint, tar, varnish, and other water-repelling applications on pruning or breakage wounds has been around for a long time. But the reasons for doing so were debunked decades ago.

Just like people, trees and shrubs have their own defence and healing mechanisms to deal with such wounds. These water-repelling applications prevent our woody plants from initiating those processes and cause the very problems they are intended to prevent, namely discouraging pathogens and insects from entering the wound sites. Moisture will often get inside anyway, which sets up conditions for general rot and disease to take hold.

Woody plants do not heal in the same way that humans do. They compartmentalize or seal off the damage by forming suberin, a lipophilic macromolecule that is a biopolyester.[12] Found in plant cell walls, it is activated when a plant is wounded. The plant literally creates a new and protective but rigid wood layer in the form of a callus that starts at the edge of the wound and gradually grows inward until the entrance wound surface is covered.[13] As the plant continues to develop, new growth will spread over the callus, but does not integrate with it. An elegant and effective process!

What we can do to assist our trees and shrubs is to prune them at the best time of the year, namely late winter and early spring, when insects and pathogens are reduced. Before pruning, water the plant well ahead of time or immediately afterward so it is well-hydrated at the time of surgery. (Only do this if the soil is thawed. Skip the watering if the ground is still frozen.) Learn the techniques of how to prune and practise on deadfall before going ahead. Avoid fertilizing the plant after pruning, especially if the fertilizer contains a high percentage of nitrogen. Then let the plant be. Just like us, it needs time and space to recover![14] —JM

Sunscald injury—what is it and how can it be prevented?

Sunscald usually occurs on the southwest side of a tree, when the winter sun stimulates cell activity within the tree's cambium (the layer facilitating movement of water and nutrients), which is then suddenly frozen by a dip in nighttime temperatures.

When you plant trees, site them so they are protected from sunscald.

You may notice the effects of sunscald after it has occurred, during the following spring or summer: the bark of affected trees may crack and peel or become discoloured. Young trees are most susceptible; older ones are protected by thicker bark. Some tree species, such as apples and crabapples, have thin bark and may be more prone to sunscald.

To reduce the risk of sunscald, purchase tree wraps or plastic guards, made of light-coloured material, to reflect the sun and to help stabilize temperatures. Place them on the trunks of trees at risk in the fall, and remove the wraps in the spring. Traditional methods of combatting sunscald include applying a whitewash made from hydrated lime (calcium hydroxide) and salt, or white interior latex paint diluted with water, but the tree wraps are inexpensive and truly less work to use (plus, whitewashing isn't recommended for very young trees, anyway).

Trees suffering from drought stress can be more prone to sunscald injury, so keep up with a regular watering schedule through the growing season. Apply a two-inch (five-centimetre) layer of organic mulch, such as wood chips, to the base of trees to help regulate soil temperatures, maintain moisture, and combat the effects of freeze-and-thaw cycles during the winter.

Heavy pruning can sometimes expose tree trunks to sunscald—something to bear in mind when you make those cuts.

Trees will usually heal on their own if the cracks aren't massive and there is no further damage inflicted by disease or pests. (A tree is highly at risk if more than 25 percent of the bark around its circumference has been removed. Then there is the potential for girdling, which can be fatal.) If there are bits of loose bark coming away from the tree, carefully trim them away with a pair of clean pruning shears or a sharp knife. This will help prevent insect pests from taking up residence behind the lifted bark, where you can't see them.[15] — SN

This crabapple tree has been severely injured by cracking due to sunscald and frost.

Should I wrap evergreens in burlap to protect them from drying out in the winter?

I really hate seeing evergreen plants all tightly wrapped up in burlap for the winter. Surely one primary reason we have evergreen species in our gardens is for winter interest with their great structures and gorgeous greens, amid all the white. So, when I see them tightly bundled up, they remind me of nothing so much as ugly candles just waiting to be lit.

That mini-rant done, I do use burlap to protect newly planted evergreens for the first couple of years while they are establishing good root systems and generally getting used to our climate, especially if they are in really exposed locations. The goal is to reduce potential sunscald, provide a windbreak from drying winds, and deter hungry critters from munching on them, while still providing them with good air circulation and not mollycoddling them.

So, in late fall before the first freeze-up, I pound in three or four stakes vertically, approximately 1 foot (0.3 metres) away from the widest points of the plant and about 1 foot (0.3 metres) taller than the top. Then, once the dangerous period comes around (January through April), I'll staple burlap tightly to the stakes, encircling the tree or shrub, and leave it there until spring and the ground defrosts. I don't want the burlap touching any of the leaves as it can wick away moisture and defeat the purpose. Nor do I want it so close it will trap moisture or heat in and encourage conditions for pathogens to set up shop.

After those first two winters, they are on their own so I can enjoy them year-round.[16] —JM

Colorado blue spruce shouldn't
be sprayed with anti-desiccants.

Are anti-desiccant sprays recommended to protect evergreens and conifers against drying winter winds?

Evergreen trees and shrubs are vulnerable to desiccation (removal of all moisture from leaves and needles) and sunscald due to warmer temperatures and drying winds. Unlike deciduous plants, they continue to transpire (uptaking water through their roots and releasing it as water vapour through their leaves) during the winter when temperatures are favourable, even after the soil has frozen. The result when direct sun and drying winds are introduced into the mix: anything from minor damage to the tips of their leaves all the way through to plant death. This applies to both broadleaf evergreens and conifers.

Anti-desiccant (or anti-transpirant) sprays can be used to shepherd evergreens and conifers safely through the winter. Made from pine oil or chemical polymers, they are sprayed onto leaves once the plants are fully dormant. The coating serves to deter transpiration and usually lasts up to four months before it wears off. In areas where winter comes early and stays longer, two applications are wise, as the extreme danger comes when the days are getting longer and warmer, but the soil is still frozen.

Wait for a day in early December, or even later if the fall has been warm, when the plant is fully dormant, meaning moisture has moved into the roots, as you don't want to trap residual moisture in the leaves where it will freeze and possibly damage the leaf tissue. Temperatures should be around 40 to 50°F (4 to 10°C) and no precipitation should be in the forecast for a couple of days. Liberally spray the leaves—both the tops and underneath.

I generally use an anti-desiccant on newly planted or young trees and shrubs for up to three years. After that they should have developed big enough root systems to hold adequate moisture for the winter. I don't bother with any plant taller or wider than me!

PS: Don't apply anti-desiccants to any plant that has its own natural waxy coating, such as the Colorado blue spruce.[17]—JM

Care and Concern

3

Why aren't my lilacs and other flowering trees and shrubs blooming?

Flowering shrubs and trees, such as lilacs, sometimes get a bit of stage fright and fail to produce their showstopping floral displays when you are eagerly anticipating them. There are several reasons why they might do this.

Did you prune at the right time last year? Some flowering trees and shrubs—lilacs and forsythia are prime examples—bloom on last year's growth. If you cut that off too late in the year, the plant will not be able to produce buds in time to hit the current year's window of bloom time. Prune shrubs and trees that bloom on old wood immediately after they flower to prevent this from occurring. And don't be too heavy-handed—a severe pruning may also be responsible for a lack of flowers.

Is your tree or shrub advanced in age? If so, it may stop blooming. For some shrubs, such as potentilla, you may be able to do a rejuvenation pruning nearly to ground level to refresh the plant. Don't expect blooms right afterward, however—it will be a couple of years' wait, at least. Many other plants cannot tolerate a hard pruning, especially when they are nearing the end of their life cycles. Just let them be.

On the other hand, is your tree or shrub fresh off the nursery lot or newly dug from the field? If so, it likely won't bloom the first year, or even the second or third. Give it a chance to establish itself.

Frost injury can be another cause of a lack of flowering—a dip into severely cold temperatures during the winter or a late spring frost are common culprits on the prairies. When siting your trees and shrubs, avoid frost pockets (low-lying areas where cold air settles). Choose fruiting plants that bloom as late in the spring as possible to avoid spring frosts. Apples and pears, for example, often bloom later than members of the *Prunus* genus, such as cherries and plums. Apricots almost always lose their flowers due to late frosts or chilling winds.

Extremely cold temperatures in winter can also damage flower buds, even though the buds seem snugly and safely ensconced. Unfortunately, there isn't anything you can do to stop this from happening.

While this lilac clearly doesn't, flowering trees and shrubs occasionally have performance anxiety. There are several factors that may contribute to their lack of flower production.

Is your tree or shrub getting enough sunlight? If not, that may be why you're not seeing many flowers. At least six hours of sunlight per day is needed for these plants to be their floriferous best!

Keep weeds from encroaching on the base of the tree or shrub. Nuff said.

Mulching your trees or shrubs is always a good idea. Drought-stressed plants will let you know they are unhappy by doing silly things like not blooming.

Did you offer a bit too much nitrogen-based fertilizer the previous growing season and then apply more this spring? If so, that may have encouraged lush vegetative growth in lieu of flower production. Remember, go easy on the fertilizing of trees and shrubs—they generally don't require much, if any, each year.

Try not to fret too much if your trees and shrubs don't bloom. Some years, environmental stresses are the major reason for this problem, and you may not be able to do anything about it. In some cases, however, if you make corrections to the way you care for the plant, you'll be rewarded with beautiful blooms.[1]—SN

Hydrangeas, like this 'Annabelle', are genuine showstoppers when they bloom!

What is tree girdling, and how do I prevent it?

The term "girdling" refers to the unfortunate circumstance when a tree branch or trunk is constricted by something that has been wrapped around it. If you've ever purchased a tree from a nursery and forgot to remove the plastic tag from the nursery attached to the tree, go out and do it now! As the plant grows, that piece of plastic can strangle the tree branch or trunk. If you need to stake your newly planted trees, to prevent girdling, don't leave the staking system in place for more than a year.

In many cases, the thing doing the girdling happens to be the tree's own roots. A main root (or roots) may grow in a circular pattern around the trunk below the soil line. As this root coils, it chokes off the flow of sap within the tree. Slowly, the tree will begin to die. The movement of water and nutrients through the tree is restricted, and you won't likely see the symptoms until a few years into the tree's decline. There may be twig or branch dieback that you cannot attribute to factors such as the weather. You may notice the canopy of the tree is starting to thin out, especially in the uppermost regions. The leaves may be lighter in colour or drop prematurely. The tree may begin to lean for no apparent reason. A tree that is stressed by girdling roots will be less resistant to pests and diseases, which will further weaken it and accelerate the decline.

The causes of tree girdling aren't always man-made. Certain diseases such as black knot (caused by the pathogen *Apiosporina morbosa*) can form growths that will strangle the tree. Wildlife, such as porcupines or deer, can eat a critical amount of bark and other tissue and girdle a tree.

Some types of trees tend to naturally girdle more than others—examples include pines, poplars, and elms. Container-grown trees also frequently exhibit girdling roots. Often, loosening and spreading apart the roots by hand at planting time is enough to prevent the problem later in the tree's life. Make sure you don't dig a cramped little hole to stuff the tree into, either—it may be extra work, but digging spacious planting holes will facilitate better spreading of the root systems (see pages 23–24).

Sometimes you can remove a girdling root while the tree is still in the ground — it depends on the size of the root and whether or not it has fused with the trunk of the tree. Consult with a certified arborist to find out if such a solution is worth undertaking. It won't be a task you can likely do yourself, and there will be factors such as cost to consider.

As an aside, you may also hear the term girdling in conjunction with forestry management. Sometimes trees are intentionally girdled as a method of control instead of cutting them down; for example, if it would be challenging to remove a tree from a protected area. In these cases, it is common to cut a ring into the tree bark to fatally wound the tissue of the phloem, xylem, and cambium, which will slowly kill the tree. (There is a related procedure called ringbarking, which removes tissue from the phloem and cambium and kills the tree even more slowly than girdling.)[2] —SN

What can I do to remove a tree stump from my yard?

Depending on where your tree stump is located, you may wish to have it removed. In some gardens, tree stumps—in particular, tall ones, which are often called snags—can be a desirable element. You may want to keep a stump around to provide a source of food for birds (the decaying wood will likely house some delicious bugs and grubs). A snag can offer cover for them to hide or even serve as a nesting cavity. Other wildlife such as bats, mice, voles, squirrels, amphibians, and reptiles may use snags for various purposes. In addition, a myriad of mosses, lichens, and fungi will use snags as a medium to grow on.

A snag can become a problem if it has decayed to a point where it may fall down or cause damage. Keeping a snag isn't for everyone, as some gardeners worry it may attract pest insects that could infest other plants in their yards. Another potential issue is the root systems of some tree species will continue to grow even after the rest of the tree has been removed. If the tree is located too close to a building or the root systems are seeking water from nearby pipes, removal is essential.

As long as shorter stumps are not in a place where they can pose tripping hazards, these stumps are sometimes left in the ground and used for decorative purposes: I've seen them serve as stands for container-grown plants or for pieces of yard art. "Stumperies" is the name given to garden features that include stumps or other pieces of dead wood.

If the tree stump in your yard is an unwanted element, an arborist can grind it out or remove it entirely. Grinding is less expensive and easier to do. A tool with rotating blades is used to chew up the stump several inches below ground level, leaving the tree's roots intact. The chips can be used for mulch, and you can plant right over the site. Removing the stump requires excavation. It may leave you with a hole in the ground and in your wallet, but it is also highly effective at dealing with the problem.[3]—SN

It is likely that the gardener saddled with this poplar stump and all its accompanying suckers will want to grind it out or remove it.

My conifer trees are turning brown. What are the possible reasons for this?

In our minds, we expect conifers to always keep their needles (aside from deciduous conifers, that is). So, what gives when they do not?

Usually they are experiencing "flagging," the seasonal drop of needles, typically in the fall. Spruce species hold their needles for three to five years, whereas pines keep theirs for two to three years, and cedars lose entire branchlets that are older. So long as new growth is occurring at the tip of the branches in the spring, there is no cause for concern.

In years when there is extreme weather, there is likely to be a heavier needle drop come fall, given the stress the plants have experienced. Additionally, events that occurred some years ago may contribute to heavy needle drop as the plant is likely using up its stored energy. Overland flooding, prolonged wet periods, drought, extreme summer heat, early heavy snowstorms in the fall, and unseasonable heat in the winter have all been experienced on the prairies in the last decade. Not surprisingly, our trees are manifesting that stress by shedding older needles.

Root damage also manifests itself with browning and the eventual loss of needles. Soil compaction, changes in water tables, improper watering and fertilization practices, too much mulch, or simply outgrowing its space and not having enough room to stretch its roots will all cause root damage and impact a plant's ability to draw up water and nutrients. Rodents and other mammals may dig under or around the base of the trunk to the point that the outer bark, the cambium, the xylem, and the phloem are damaged, which will affect the ability of the roots to function properly. Pathogens such as root rot in cedars are a particular concern.

Improper planting and transplant shock in newly planted specimens can also be the problem, and that shock can manifest itself a few years down the road—not just the first season—particularly if the tree is planted too deeply or if the roots were not spread out when planted to prevent girdling.

Up top, suspect herbicide drift if the brown area is on just one side, or dog urine if the patch is lower down. If the plant is too close to a wall or a fence where little light can reach the dark side, there will be considerable needle drop as the needles there cannot photosynthesize properly.

Most often, we think an insect or a pathogen is the culprit, so once other causes are eliminated, do check for signs of eggs, larvae, or adult insects on the plant. Webbing, frass (the excretion of insect larvae), and chewed needles are also indications of insect trouble. Symptoms of possible pathogens include drooping branchlets, fruiting bodies of fungi, and oozing of sap on the trunk or branches. If any of these are found, it is time to call in expert help to confirm the diagnosis and institute a remediation regimen.

Conifers can recover but only if the cause(s) is correctly identified and if there are realistic ways to provide what the tree needs to overcome the problem.[4]—JM

These ground cover junipers are suffering from a combination of winter desiccation and the inadvertent application of sidewalk salt.

My tree or shrub has experienced dieback. What causes this, and is there anything I can do about it?

Dieback, the death of tree twigs and limbs, shrub stems, and roots, can be caused by a multitude of issues. It is a symptom of many diseases caused by pathogens and insects, as well as improper planting; mechanical damage; lack of nutrients; pollution, including salt damage; weather events, such as droughts and floods; and extreme conditions in winter. It can even occur simply because, due to old age, the plant is dying.

It is never wise to make assumptions about the cause of dieback, as there can be multiple issues stressing the plant that may be cumulative. In many instances, the original stressor is soil degradation impacting root systems, mechanical injury to upper limbs, an adverse weather occurrence, an insect infestation, or a combination of several events. Secondary biotic or abiotic agents may further weaken the plant, and there may be other events that finally damage it sufficiently for it to decline and die. It is imperative to try to diagnose the causes in order to attempt to remediate growing conditions and/or manage the pathogens or pests. It is difficult to reverse dieback, but it is always worth a try! The key is to always monitor your plants and be able to detect changes for the worse. Take action right away—as soon as you notice something is wrong. Best of all is prevention, which starts with purchasing healthy plants, matching them to the conditions they need to thrive, and ensuring they are planted correctly.

Some years otherwise healthy trees and shrubs suffer from winterkill, due to not being fully dormant before the arrival of a sudden and deep freeze. Dieback can also occur after a warm period, followed by a descent back into winter. It is a deep mystery to me how our woody plants can survive all that winter throws at them, but key to that success is their ability to withdraw water from their cells, leaving an elevated level of sugars and salts that act like antifreeze as temperatures drop. Water is literally drawn from inside the cell walls to outside them. If there is a sudden, rapid, and deep freeze (which often happens on the prairies) before the plant is in full dormancy, then ice can form inside the cell walls, leading to cell death, which we see as blackened stems and limbs, come spring.

The remedy is to prune back the dead stems and limbs to the first live bud. For shrubs that may see winterkill, that can be down to the snow cover level or to the crown of the shrub. Give the plant a lot of TLC and let it resume growth, and then train it back to how it looked before dieback occurred.[5] —JM

This Schubert chokecherry has suffered some dieback due to harsh winter weather.

Do poplars and other types of trees break water pipes and foundations if they are sited too close to them?

The urban legend around poplar trees invading our water and sewer pipes and creating devastation all around is like most legends, based in both reality and myth.

The myth is that roots can break pipes and foundations. I always have this mental image of a *Lord of the Rings* Ent running rampant in my garden, smashing rock and foundations alike! The reality is that roots are tasked with the job of bringing in the water, air, and nutrients needed for plants, and some woody species have large root systems — indeed, up to two and a half times the height of a plant at maturity. The roots have an incredible ability to seek out sources of water, air, and nutrients and, without fail, will head in that direction.

Our pipes have been made from either concrete or Orangeburg "no-corrode" sewer piping (up until the 1970s), clay tile (until the late 1980s), or more recently polyvinyl chloride (PVC). To a greater or lesser extent, these pipes allow the necessities of life to escape through their pores, with PVC being the most impervious. In many instances, roots will bind tightly to the pipes to take advantage of the water source that they need, and they can exert tremendous pressure on pipes. Roots will naturally take advantage of degrading pipes that have been flexed as they go through multiple freeze-and-thaw cycles and have developed leaks or joints. That goes for foundations with cracks that are another source of air and humidity and for the weeping tile that drains away water from house foundations.

The fine roots will enter the pipes and set up shop, until you notice slowing drainage in sinks or toilets, and/or backup in drains in basements from washing machines. The homeowner then must root out the roots. Since pipes are considered private property, the homeowner is responsible in most cases for the damage, no matter whose tree may be the culprit.

The good news is there are techniques and methods to prevent the damage, short of digging up everything and reinstalling your pipes:

* When considering planting woody plants, get a map of where the water and sewer pipes are located. Any large tree or shrub should be sited at least ten feet (three metres) away from the pipes and/or the foundation.
* If you are constructing a home, redoing your landscaping, or replacing pipes, have them coated in a compound that makes them more impervious.
* Know the species that have large root systems, and perhaps consider an alternative.
* Have a regular television inspection of your pipes to make sure you haven't developed a root problem, and, if you have, know that it can be worked on before it causes really big and expensive problems.
* Roots can be regularly flushed out, and there are products to deter root growth inside pipes. Some are more dangerous to the environment than others.

In descending order of being problematic species, the Big Five are: poplar, willow, elm, ash, and birch, all of which are commonly used in parks, boulevards, and gardens as they are fast growing, are inexpensive, and create a great urban canopy. Be aware, though, that all tree and shrub roots are going to go where the going is good—right to your pipes![6]—JM

I need to cut down a poplar tree. How can I minimize the number of suckers that will form?

Poplars and aspens, members of the genus *Populus*, are fast-growing softwood species, well-known for spreading through colonization. Genetically, they are predisposed to send up suckers from growth points along their extensive root systems, essentially propagating vegetatively as clones. Well-established groves have a huge biomass of roots with identical trees growing from such a system.

All of which is to say that eliminating such a tree from your garden is not a simple matter of removing the upper structures and expecting that the root system will slowly rot away. No matter what you do, the tree will seek to re-establish itself by sending up suckers at many points along its roots. The goal is to reduce the number of suckers as they come up and to eliminate the energy residing in the root system that will be focused on growing those suckers!

Start by cutting down the main trunk when it is fully leafed out, say in June or July, as a lot of the energy stored when the tree was dormant in the fall and the winter has been used to grow leaves.

At the same time, remove as many of the main roots as you can. I remember when I cut my poplar down, we excavated just about the whole yard! That isn't always possible, but it really helped reduce the suckering.

Then, whenever you see a sucker coming up, dig it out right away before it gets a chance to establish. If you can get down to where it attaches to the root and roughly rip it out, it won't regrow there again. Some people simply mow the suckers as they arise, which works too but leaves a bit to continue photosynthesizing. After a year (or two), you will have reduced the energy enough that the root system will start to decompose and will eventually disappear.

Some people advocate using poison to kill off the roots, either by painting it onto the suckers or by applying it to the trunk. I always worry the poison will translocate through the roots and be absorbed by desired plants. Poison in the soil will also affect soil life and potentially wildlife. Instead, I strongly encourage the slow-and-steady path.[7] —JM

What is the difference between water sprouts and suckers?

Suckers and water sprouts are epicormic shoots that seemingly grow for no good reason, either at the base of a tree's trunk or its crown, or right out of the trunk, or along its branches. They grow extremely fast and straight up, reaching for the sun. They often have overly large leaves. They spring up from dormant growth buds that suddenly become active due to pruning cuts, breakage from storms, overall stress, or overfertilization.

Suckers are shoots generated from the rootstock of the plant, either along underground nodes of the lateral roots or close to the surface, right where the flare of the trunk or the crown of the shrub meets the ground. It is a form of vegetative reproduction, and some trees and shrubs, such as colonizing genera like *Populus* (aspens and poplars) and *Rubus* (which includes raspberries and blackberries), are genetically prone to this type of growth. Chokecherry (*Prunus virginiana*) shrubs, Schubert chokecherry (*P. virginiana* 'Schubert') trees, and mayday (*Prunus padus*) trees are also (in)famous for suckering. Most woody plants will sucker if under stress, whether from drought, damage to the plant above, or impairment to the root system.

Water sprouts are shoots growing from above-ground growth nodes and are weakly attached to where they originated. Most trees and shrubs will generate them when stressed, especially when they are incorrectly pruned or have suffered damage.

Both water sprouts and suckers can interfere with the structure of a tree, and we often think of them as disfigurements. Prune them off in the spring when you first spot them, making sure to not leave the growth node behind to regrow. Then assess the plant to see if you can determine the reason for the suckers or water sprouts to remedy the issue.[8]—**JM**

This chokecherry is overrun with suckers.

The growth generated by water sprouts is weak. Prune them off if you spot them.

71

My fruit trees are heavy producers some years, and in other years, the yield is very poor. Why is this happening?

Large fruit trees such as apples, pears, and plums often experience biennial bearing or alternate bearing. This means these species set their fruit buds in the current year for flowering and also begin the process of setting fruit for the next season. Simply put, in one year a tree may expend such large amounts of energy into maturing its fruit that there is little left over for setting fruit buds for the following year, and much smaller yields of fruit are then produced.

To ensure you do not get such imbalances of production, the trick (if you can make yourself do it!) is to thin out immature fruit within a critical time frame of two weeks to one month after the tree has flowered. The usual rule is one fruit per cluster, which really hurts but over time will become easier as you start to achieve consistent yields.[9]—**JM**

This looks like an indicator of a decent apple crop!

My apple tree just dropped a bunch of fruit on the ground—and it's only early summer! Why did it do this?

Don't freak out! Apple trees naturally release some unripe fruit in mid-summer— it's called "June drop," even though it can take place in either June or July. (The usual timing is six to eight weeks after flowering.) You may notice young apple trees seem to shed more fruit than older trees.

There are a couple of reasons for June drop. Sometimes poor weather (too hot, too cold, too wet, too dry) will be responsible. Most often, it has to do with carbohydrates—no, really! Just like we can become overloaded with pasta and bread and need a break from carbohydrates, so, too, can an apple tree (well, sort of). What happens is that the production of fruit greatly outmatches the amount of leaf surface in the tree canopy, which struggles to keep up with its photosynthesizing duties. Something has to give, so the tree "thins" itself. June drop is also a measure of protection for the upcoming harvest: it prevents the tree from producing an excessive amount of fruit, which could potentially weigh down the branches and cause breakage.

There isn't any need to worry about June drop. If your tree sheds a huge amount of apples each year, and it seems to be affecting the amount you are able to harvest, try the following suggestions:

* Prune the tree to allow more light to penetrate the canopy. The best time to do this is in March or early April, before the flower buds open.
* Avoid applications of high-nitrogen fertilizer. However, a side-dressing of compost in the spring is useful.
* Keep up with a regular watering schedule, particularly if the spring and the early summer are dry.
* Mulch the base of your trees.[10] —SN

Why aren't my fruit trees producing fruit?

There are a few reasons why your fruit trees may not be bearing fruit. On the prairies, damage to flower buds from late spring frosts is a common problem that home gardeners cannot do a lot to prevent. But one thing we *can* do is not site our trees and shrubs at the base of slopes, which may trap frigid air.

Sometimes, when a fruit tree is overfertilized with nitrogen, it will fail to produce fruit. More is not better when it comes to fertilizing. Go easy on the fertilizer, particularly the high-nitrogen stuff—trees and shrubs really don't need a lot of it.

Pruning is another reason why fruit production may be puny. If you are heavy-handed with the loppers in the late winter, your fruit trees may sulk. When pruning, never remove more than a quarter of the canopy.

The age of the tree or the shrub can be another reason for poor fruit production. If the plant is reaching the end of its life cycle, it may no longer be inclined to fruit. If the tree or shrub is young or newly planted, give it time to establish before expecting fruit. Peak production often doesn't happen a year or two after planting—it can take years for some species.

Pollination—either the kind that fails to occur or the kind that isn't very efficient—is often to blame when fruit trees do not produce fruit. When you purchase your plants, check to see if they are self-fertile or require pollinizers (compatible varieties of plants for cross-pollination). Most apples need a pollinizer, as do pears and haskap berries. The bloom period of both plants must overlap to increase the success rate of cross-pollination. If that additional plant isn't present nearby, your tree may bear flowers annually, but no fruit.

You also need pollinators to work for your fruit trees. Many fruit trees are pollinated by insects, so encouraging a healthy population of bees to your garden is essential.

With fruit trees, the gardener needs to exercise a bit of care and attention. Trees and shrubs that are stressed by improper planting practices, overcrowding, and just plain inappropriate siting may simply decide enough is enough. When you plant your trees and shrubs, remember the old adage "Right plant, right place."[11] —SN

No issues with pollination (or anything else)
for these Nanking cherries!

The ground is frozen, and we've had snow, but my deciduous tree hasn't lost all of its leaves. Is this a sign there is something wrong with my tree?

Chances are, your tree is fine. In response to autumn's colder temperatures, deciduous trees start manufacturing specialized abscission cells that facilitate the shedding of leaves. When plants drop their leaves, they no longer need to provide water to the leaves, which means less moisture will be lost as the trees go through dormancy. Frost damage is also minimized by the shedding of leaves. Most of the time, trees manage to accomplish the creation of abscission cells and the leaves fall before the truly cold, winter-like weather settles in. But when we have warm weather late into the fall, and then a prolonged spell of freezing temperatures occurs very suddenly, the leaves are not ready to drop yet because those cells haven't been produced. The leaves then freeze on the trees and often stick around all winter.

The following spring, they'll slough off when the new buds appear, and the trees leaf out. Microclimates can also influence how quickly trees accomplish abscission, so some trees of the same species in the same yard may successfully drop all of their leaves and others may not.

Usually, the only time this becomes a problem is when we have an extremely wet, heavy snowfall and the weight of it on the persistent leaves can cause some branches to break.[12] —SN

This beautiful forsythia shrub is blooming in early spring, and you can still see last year's leaves on the plant. There is nothing wrong with this.

My trees are really late leafing out in the spring. What causes this, and is there anything I can do about it?

Most of the time, when trees and shrubs leaf out late in the spring—or worse, don't leaf out at all—the weather is to blame. (I particularly like this excuse because it takes a huge amount of blame off the gardener!) Severe dips in temperature and abrupt freeze-and-thaw cycles in the winter, as well as late frosts in the spring, are obvious culprits. If your plants have just come through a year or two of drought, that can also contribute to the problem. The opposite is also true; most trees and shrubs don't care much for sitting in a bog and will let you know they're unhappy.

Tailor your tree and shrub care to combat these issues. Make sure you decide on the right place to plant your tree or shrub before you haul out your credit card and bring the plant home from the nursery. Don't cram it in any old place where it sort of fits. Think about the mature size of the tree and how much space and light it will need to thrive, not merely subsist. Consider the health of your soil where you want to plant it. Trees and shrubs aren't cookies—they aren't all stamped from the same mould. They all have different needs, and you must cater to them if you want your plant to flourish.

Carefully plant your trees so the roots do not girdle. You can read our tips on how to prevent tree girdling on pages 61–62.

Use mulch to help conserve moisture at the base of the plant—a boon during dry seasons. Mulch will also help protect your trees and shrubs from freeze-and-thaw cycles in the winter.

If your tree is late to leaf out, don't jump to conclusions and immediately yank it out. If the plant is still showing signs of life (the branches aren't brittle and don't break easily when very gently bent), hang on. It might take a full year or more for recovery, but give the tree the time it needs to bounce back.[13] —SN

An early snowstorm brought extremely heavy, wet snow and broke several tree branches. What do I do now?

If the trees have hit utility lines, call the authorities for help. Do everything you can to stay safe. Seeing the damage is heartbreaking, but let the snow melt away from the branches before you take any other action. (Get on the phone and make an appointment with a certified arborist if it looks like you'll need one, but otherwise try to be patient.)

The good news? Bent branches will often rebound, so there is no need to do anything to correct them. Allow nature to take its course. If less than half of the tree limbs have snapped off, or they are small branches, the tree may make a recovery if pruned properly. In such a case, the arborist you just called will be able to get a crew in to help save your tree. And young, newly planted trees may recover—even if they have fallen down. Secure them back into the planting hole and, if possible, stake them to prevent further upturning. (They can remain staked for one year after planting.)

Shrubs often rebound more readily than trees from storm damage. If they are encased in ice, allow it to melt. Heavy snow may be carefully brushed off with a broom, but remember to brush upwards instead of downwards to prevent further breakage of branches. Pruning the plants in the spring may correct much of the damage, although the shrubs may look a bit awkward for a time, and they may not bloom or produce fruit that year. For both trees and shrubs, be careful not to prune off too much, as the plants will need as much of their foliage as possible to help heal themselves in the coming year.

The bad news? If more than 50 percent of the tree's crown has been ripped off, or more than half of the tree limbs (especially large ones) have been broken, the tree isn't likely to survive. For conifers, in particular, if the leader has been broken, the tree may not recover. (Deciduous trees may fare better.) And if your tree has been torn up from the ground and more than a third of its roots are exposed, it's probably a goner. Consult with your arborist, but get ready for the news that your tree may need to be removed.

Sometimes it's not worth saving a damaged tree, especially if it was already affected by another issue such as disease or was planted in a site where it simply didn't fit (perhaps it was too close to power lines or another building or was casting too much shade, due to its mature size). A tree that has suffered storm damage may be weakened by the experience and could come down in another storm. You could be liable for the cost of damages if that tree hits your neighbour's roof or their car.[14] —SN

Unusually heavy snow isn't the only weather event that can break large tree branches. Heavy winds and hail can do similar damage.

Pests and Diseases

4

We focused on many common (and a few not-so-common!) diseases and wildlife and insect pests affecting plants in our book *The Prairie Gardener's Go-To for Pests and Diseases* (2020), but we'd be remiss if we didn't cover in this book some of the biggies that can cause problems for trees and shrubs in prairie gardens. From oystershell scale and black knot fungus to those troublesome leaf-and-stem-sucking aphids and bark-munching porcupines, you need to be able to accurately identify what you're seeing with (or on!) your trees and shrubs, so you can attempt to control or treat the issue, if necessary. To help you find the information you're looking for, we've grouped the questions to address insect pests first, then diseases, and finally wildlife pests.

Bear in mind not everything wrong with your trees and shrubs is due to a creepy-crawly, a furry culprit, a fungal spore, or microscopic bacterium—many times, there is an abiotic factor at play. These include stresses that can be blamed on the weather or nutrient deficiencies in your soil. There are also problems associated with mechanical injury, such as someone accidentally bashing the blade of a lawn mower against a tree trunk. Chemical injury—usually due to herbicide drift—is another unfortunate possibility.

Once you've determined what is going on with your trees and shrubs, it's time to decide if you need to take action. Often, problems are not severe enough to warrant doing anything—the damage might be cosmetic in nature, and, while we hate seeing our plants looking their least attractive, chances are, given a bit of time, they will fully recover. We simply have to understand and accept that in a thriving, living ecosystem, plants may get eaten or damaged by something. Our goal is to try to provide the best possible care for the plants in our gardens and ensure they are healthy enough to ward off or sustain attacks from pests and diseases.

Unfortunately, no matter what you do to prevent problems, there may come a time when your trees and shrubs can't stand up to an onslaught of trouble, and you stand to lose them if you don't do something. Sometimes the actions we can take are simple, such as putting up a wire tree guard to keep voles from chewing on the bark of a tree in the winter, or spraying hordes of aphids out of a tree canopy with a strong blast of water from a garden hose. Other times, it pays to consult a certified arborist. They have the knowledge and experience to identify problems and determine how to deal with them. If you don't know what is wrong with your trees and shrubs, and have no clue how to manage whatever it is, obtain help from a professional. The website for the International Society of Arboriculture (isa-arbor.com) is a useful resource and hosts a list of certified arborists in your area. — SN

When do I need to call a certified arborist for help?

Sometimes, when it comes to tree and shrub troubles, you can't go it alone; you need the assistance of an expert. Here is a list of some common occurrences when putting in a call to an arborist is likely necessary:

* Your tree has fallen or suffered severe damage due to a storm or other event. (If there are power lines involved, phone the utility company first.)
* The roots of your tree are suddenly exposed (ripped up).
* Your mature tree is leaning.
* Your tree is cracked or split.
* There are cavities forming in your tree.
* Your tree or shrub is suffering from a pest issue or disease requiring diagnosis and treatment.
* Your tree or shrub has girdled roots.
* Your tree or shrub requires pruning for aesthetic purposes or regular maintenance.
* You can't do the job on your own. It's okay if you don't have the knowledge or experience to look after your trees or shrubs. The plant may be so large that you can't physically or safely undertake the task, and you may not have the proper equipment to do so.

A certified arborist is one who has been credentialed by a regulatory body such as the International Society of Arboriculture (ISA). Look for certified arborists in your area by using the list on the ISA website (isa-arbor.com). — **SN**

*Not all caterpillars are the bad
guys, but they do need to eat!*

There are caterpillars chowing down on the leaves of my trees and shrubs. How do I boot them out of the banquet?

Caterpillars are the larval form of moths and butterflies. If you love and respect the adult insects as beneficial pollinators, you may have to squelch your hatred for the voraciously feeding young 'uns and let them munch away on at least a few of your plants. (Of course, not all caterpillars turn into lovely helpful beneficials—white cabbage moths are a prime example, as are those positively nasty cutworms that take out seedlings with impunity. And then there are tent caterpillars. The memories of their frequent summertime appearances when I was a child in northern Alberta still give me the crawlies.) With caterpillars, you need to identify them accurately so you know whether you are dealing with a friend or foe. If you can't figure it out yourself, find an expert who can. Not all caterpillars need controlling—and if the damage is only to a few plants and largely cosmetic, there is no need to take any action.

Damage from caterpillars on trees and shrubs is typically on leafy surfaces and stems. You'll notice ragged chunks ripped out of leaves or entire leaves missing. Some caterpillars, such as tent and ugly nest, will leave telltale webbing as they move around and feed. You'll also see the creatures in question—most caterpillars tend to be fairly easy to spot as they steadily chow down.

If you can reach the caterpillars, you can hand-pick them off of your shrubs and trees with gloved hands or a soft, damp cloth. Dislodging them with water from the garden hose may also work. And encourage birds to your yard at all times. Many species, such as chickadees, nuthatches, and grosbeaks, absolutely adore eating caterpillars. You can't do any better than this free form of pest control.

After a caterpillar infestation, treat your stressed trees and shrubs with a lot of TLC. Ensure they are watered properly and not subjected to drought. Do not prune them that year if you don't absolutely need to—give them a chance to recover. Hold off on the fertilizer. And be patient; a severe attack may put a dent in flower, fruit, and seed production that year. Generally, however, the plants will be fine, if given time, and if they are not subsequently harmed by another pest or disease.—SN

Aphids have invaded my trees and shrubs. What can I do?

Aphids feed in massive clusters (usually numbering in what looks like the zillions). They are tiny flightless insects with pear-shaped bodies. They can be black, green, grey, brown, red, or white in colour. Different species of aphids target specific host plants—and there are so many types, there are few plants exempt from their attacks. They have sucking mouthparts and take up the juices from stems and leaves of plants, which causes the leaves to become stippled and turn yellow. Eventually, the foliage curls and dries out. As aphids slurp up the plant juices, they excrete a sugary liquid called honeydew. Sometimes, groups of ants will march up and down a tree in search of honeydew. Don't target the ants as pests—they are not attacking your trees or shrubs. If you get rid of the aphids, the ants will tootle away to another location.

Even if they number in the infinitesimal, aphids seldom do permanent damage to a tree or shrub. What they can do, however, is stress and weaken the plant so it becomes more susceptible to diseases and other attacks from pests.

Control aphids by violently ousting them from the plant with a powerful blast of water from the garden hose. You can also use a soft, damp cloth or your gloved hands to gently wipe the insects off the plant (of course, you can't necessarily reach every spot on your tree or shrub, but this effort can at least get rid of several thousand of them). Frequently repeat your endeavours until you notice the numbers decline.—SN

Are there any ways to treat scale insects on my trees and shrubs?

There are many types of scale insects on the prairies, but many gardeners are most familiar with oystershell scale, which targets shrubs such as cotoneasters, as well as apple and crabapple trees. European elm scale is another baddie that has done massive damage to our beautiful boulevard elms in urban areas.

There are two types of scale insects: soft scale and armored scale. Oystershell and elm scale insects fall into the latter category. We don't usually notice scale adult males as they are not the ones doing the damage. They are extremely small and they can fly. The sexually immature nymphs, referred to as "crawlers," are the ones to watch for. Armored scale insect nymphs create a hard, waxy covering to protect themselves from predators as they creep over twigs and leaves and use their piercing, sucking mouthparts to feed on plant sap. (Soft scale insects make themselves a protective coating that is fuzzy in appearance.) In oystershell scale insects, this armor looks like an oyster shell and can completely coat the surface of the stems. The adult females eventually lose their legs and become immobile on the plant until they die, but, in the meantime, they can breed and lay eggs!

The relentless chewing from hundreds of tiny larvae can cause a plant's leaves to appear stippled; the foliage may also turn yellow and drop. Like aphids, soft scale insects, such as those that infest elm trees, can produce honeydew, which can lead to another issue when a fungus called sooty mould grows on the plant surfaces that have been dripped on.

The armor the insects make is incredibly difficult to penetrate, even with insecticides. Therefore, I strongly recommend not hauling out a chemical to treat them. Some gardeners attempt pre-emptive strikes by using dormant-season horticultural oils, but timing is important when applying them. (Be sure to read and follow all of the package guidelines, and use the product that is right for your particular issue.)

Shrubs such as cotoneaster that are heavily infested with oystershell scale may be cut almost to ground level for rejuvenation. While this can suspend scale activity for a few years, the insects usually return. Ladybugs and some parasitoid wasps are effective biological controls for scale insects, so I recommend making your garden hospitable to these beneficials and letting them do the work for you.[1] —SN

While cotoneaster shrubs are highly susceptible to oystershell scale infestations, other plants such as maples (shown here), willows, poplars, lilacs, and dogwoods may also be affected.

Leaf miners have made their telltale tunnels in the leaves of my trees and shrubs. What can I do about this?

These tiny yellow or green larvae belong to several different species of butterflies and moths, and their main claim to fame is that instead of chewing on entire leaf surfaces, they mine their food from between the leaf tissues, creating highly visible tunnel patterns.

Leaf miner damage is usually cosmetic, but if an infestation is severe enough, it can stress the tree or shrub so much that they are susceptible to other pests and diseases. Clean up leaf litter in the fall to prevent the insects from overwintering. As the insects are holed up inside the leaves, chemical sprays are not able to reach them. If you have the time and inclination to do a rather unappealing task (and your affected tree or shrub is short enough that you can reach it), you can actually squish the larvae as they sup by applying pressure with your fingers on the leaves—gross, but effective. Or look for tiny rows of rice-like eggs on the undersides of leaves and gently scrape them off.[2]—SN

The tunnels created by leaf miners in plant leaves are easy to spot.

Leafrollers are a huge problem in my trees this year. Should I take action?

Every year, in mid-summer, the leaves in an aspen grove in a park by my home start to roll up like fat cigars, and if you lift one up and peer into the hollow, you might see a caterpillar either feeding or pupating. Leafrollers are the larvae of a few different species of moths, and they can be annoying, but not hugely damaging. If you tried to prune off all the affected leaves, you'd probably do serious harm to the tree's ability to efficiently photosynthesize, and you can't hand-pick the larvae or spray them due to that handy little sleeping bag they've manufactured for themselves. Don't fret about leafrollers, but try to minimize the stress they can cause on your trees. Keep up with watering when needed and don't overfertilize. — SN

Their living arrangements are not terribly attractive, but leafrollers don't tend to do significant damage to trees.

How can I treat the borers that have decided to attack my trees and shrubs?

This sizable category of insects includes the larvae of various species of moths, wasps, and beetles. I should acknowledge that not all moths, wasps, and beetles are pests! Some are predators of bugs we really don't like, some are pollinators, and some are incredibly useful for maintaining soil health. This is another reason to know exactly what you are looking at before you decide you need to treat or control it. The pests we are concerned with here are the ones that, by the way they feed, can seriously harm your trees and shrubs.

Borer larvae resemble small worms and can be different colours (usually white, green, or yellowish). They burrow into plant tissue (leaves, roots, bark, and stems) and munch away with remarkable speed, wreaking extra havoc by inviting all sorts of infection and decay to the party. Severe infestations of certain types of borers can lead to girdling and the eventual death of a tree. (Call your arborist if you suspect an out-of-control problem with borers.)

Hand-picking and washing borer larvae from plants doesn't work, as the larvae take up residency beneath the surface of plant parts. Birds can reach the insects and will happily pull them out to dine, so it may be prudent to encourage birds to your yard as a natural pest control. The most important thing you can do is to try to keep your trees and shrubs as healthy as possible, as borers tend to go after trees that are on the decline. Vigorous trees in excellent condition are not as attractive to them.[3] —SN

Leafhoppers are everywhere! What can I do to get rid of these troublesome pests?

These very small, very bouncy insects look a bit like wedge-shaped grasshoppers. You'll instantly know you're dealing with leafhoppers when you disturb a group because they will all hop everywhere at once. Leafhoppers suck the juices from plant leaves and cause the foliage and stems to distort and curl. As they feed on multiple plants, leafhoppers can spread diseases, which can lead to additional problems.

Like aphids, leafhoppers can produce honeydew, which can attract ants . . . so if you see ants kicking around your plants, chances are you have either leafhoppers or aphids (or both!) gathered in large numbers on the vegetation. The ants aren't the real problem here; they're just being opportunistic.

Leafhoppers absolutely love new lush growth, and if you are leaning heavily on nitrogen-rich fertilizers, you're just asking for leafhoppers to come around and sample the resulting fresh green succulent stems and leaves. If you're over-fertilizing, cut way back—or evaluate whether you need to use fertilizer at all. For trees and shrubs, if your soil is in good shape, you really don't need to offer them anything.

Ladybugs and green lacewings will dispatch huge numbers of leafhoppers free of charge, so make sure these beneficials have a safe, chemical-free space in your garden. Let these voracious predators do their jobs and chow down. Don't disturb lacewing cocoons if you manage to spot them, and don't freak out if you see the tank-like larvae of either insect—they are definitely the good guys.

As with aphids, repeatedly using strong jets of water from the garden hose may knock leafhoppers off and away from your plants.[4] —SN

Sowbugs are fascinating creatures! Their presence near your tree or shrub may be an indicator that the plant is on the decline. Or maybe you simply have some delectable wood mulch on the site . . .

Why do I have bugs that look like trilobites around the base of my trees and shrubs?

Chances are those weird-looking beings are European sowbugs (*Oniscus asellus*). They are also called woodlice or isopods. You might think they are insects, but they are actually crustaceans, and together with their cousins the pill bugs (*Armadillidium vulgare*), they are the only crustaceans on Earth to live entirely on land. An introduced species from Europe, they are scavengers of decaying organic matter and prefer damp and dark environments. You know you have a sowbug if it rolls up into a C-shape. It's a pill bug if it can completely roll up.

If you are seeing them at the base of a woody plant, chances are the plant is in trouble or dying. Sowbugs will live in cracks and crevices in the wood where there is both shelter and food.

Check your tree or shrub when you see them scurrying around where the trunk or stems are meeting the soil for signs and symptoms of pathogens or for other insects causing the decline of the plant. Investigate whether there have been alterations in your garden that have caused stress on the plant. Reflect on any large weather events that may have triggered a problem. If possible, prepare a plan to remediate the problem and hopefully save your plant.

Don't blame the poor sowbug or pill bug, though—they are merely doing their job of cleaning up the environment![5]—**JM**

The leaves of my trees and shrubs are covered in powdery mildew. Are there any ways to prevent this from happening next year?

Powdery mildew (*Sphaerotheca fuliginea*) is a fungus spread by the wind and is most prevalent when humidity is moderate to high and temperatures are hovering between 60 and 85°F (15.5 to 29°C). Vegetable gardeners, particularly those who grow squash, are very familiar with powdery mildew's dusty white-grey appearance on the leaves (and sometimes the stems) of plants, but it also affects a wide range of shrubs and some trees. The leaves may eventually turn yellow, then brown, and drop early. Naturally, this is very stressful for the plant.

Good air circulation can help prevent powdery mildew infections. If the canopy of your shrubs and trees is very dense, the fungus will easily spread from leaf to leaf. Prune judiciously to reduce the density of the foliage. Site your plants so they receive sufficient sunlight. The light should penetrate the canopy of the plant—if it doesn't, you have another reason to make some thinning cuts.

If your shrubs and trees end up contracting powdery mildew, remove the affected leaves. Ensure you clean up the debris from the leaves and the fruit as it falls to prevent the spread of the fungal spores.

It may sound strange, but a shrub or tree that doesn't receive enough water is more susceptible to powdery mildew, due to the severe strain that it undergoes when it is drought-stressed. If there isn't enough rainfall in your region, be sure to offer your shrubs and trees supplemental irrigation.

Finally, there are several plants that have powdery mildew–resistant cultivars–look for them when you are shopping for trees and shrubs.[6]—SN

Caraganas are susceptible to powdery mildew attacks.

In the wintertime, it is easy to spot galls caused by black knot.

My chokecherry and cherry trees have black knot. Is there something I can do to keep the fungus from killing the tree?

Black knot fungus (*Apiosporina morbosa*) is recognizable by its swollen, elongated black galls that have earned it the scatological nickname of "poop on a stick." It is hideous and deadly, as it constricts a tree's branches and trunks and limits the movement of nutrients and water through the tree. You will find it only on *Prunus* species such as chokecherry, mayday tree, Amur cherry, sour cherry, sand cherry, Nanking cherry, flowering plum, and pin cherry. The only way to remove black knot is to cut out all knot-bearing substances, and, even then, if there is enough of it, your tree may die in a few years. Make your pruning cuts approximately eight inches (twenty centimetres) below the base of the gall. Sterilize your pruning tools after each cut with full-strength rubbing alcohol, and destroy the cut branches, as the galls on them can keep producing live spores for up to four months after they have been lopped off.[7] —SN

When pruning diseased wood, ensure your pruning tools are sterilized.

Should I sterilize my pruning tools? If so, with what?

It has long been thought (and taught) that it is essential to sterilize your pruning tools whenever you set out to trim a tree or a shrub—for every single cut, no matter if the plant is diseased or not—but research has shown there are only a few times when sterilization is actually necessary. You do not need to sterilize your tools if the plant you are cutting is healthy and disease-free. Sterilization must be done if you're dealing with pathogens, from fungal or bacterial cankers, or anything attacking the vascular system of the tree. As well, if you are pruning trees or shrubs suffering from a virus, you should sterilize your tools. Dunk your pruners in undiluted isopropyl alcohol or a mouthwash containing 26.9 percent alcohol (yes, it's unconventional, and the tools—and the plant—certainly don't need the eucalyptus oil or menthol, but it is suitable for the task, and you likely have a bottle in the bathroom).[8]—SN

My tree has fire blight. Is there anything that can be done to save it?

There are many types of blights and cankers that affect plants. One of the worst is fire blight. This is a very serious, usually deadly, bacterial blight affecting members of the rose family, such as crabapples, apples, cherries, pears, cotoneasters, hawthorns, and saskatoons. Trees and shrubs affected by fire blight will look like their tips have been burned; the blackened cankers will also cause curvature in the ends of twigs and branches. You may hear it referred to as resembling a shepherd's crook. The blight will creep inward along the stems from the tips of the plant, girdling as it goes. The uptake of nutrients and water through all parts of the tree will be affected.

Fire blight, unfortunately, spreads easily from tree to tree via wind and rain. Pruning out the cankers can extend the life of your tree or shrub, but it may not save it. You must make pruning cuts at least twenty-four inches (sixty centimetres) below the canker. Do not dispose of any of the diseased material in the compost. Sterilize your pruning tools with full-strength rubbing alcohol between cuts.

Look for fire blight–resistant cultivars when shopping for trees and shrubs. If you are truly concerned, avoid species from the rose family.[9] —SN

Rust is disfiguring my trees and shrubs. Is there an effective way to deal with it?

There are many types of rusts that affect trees and shrubs, and most are host-specific. One of the most common types prairie gardeners may face is cedar-apple rust, caused by the fungus *Gymnosporangium juniperi-virginianae*. There are other rust-causing fungi closely related to this mouthful, but the standout quality of these rusts is they need two hosts to complete their life cycle: a deciduous one, such as an apple, crabapple, hawthorn, or saskatoon, and an evergreen one, such as a juniper.

This fungus tends to pop out after early summer rains, and if your neighbour's trees are sporting it, then yours likely will as well—the spores are carried along with water. If you spot brown globs on your junipers that later turn into bright orange, spiky, gelatinous balls, then turn your attention to your deciduous host— an apple, perhaps. The leaves will have spots on them that start out as a dusty yellow, then turn orange, and eventually blacken. If you flip the leaves over and check the undersides, you'll see tiny rod-like pustules, poking up from the surface.

While you can prune out the affected areas on both your deciduous and coniferous hosts, the rust will simply keep making an appearance year after year. Removal of one of the hosts is a solution, but if there are several gardens on your block that have the secondary host, you may still have issues. Fortunately, this rust is largely cosmetic, although it can weaken the trees and shrubs it affects and make them more susceptible to other problems. When planting trees and shrubs, look for rust-resistant cultivars. Make sure you clean up all leaf and fruit litter. Promote good air circulation—don't space your trees and shrubs too closely together, and if you see their canopies are getting thick and overgrown, give them a thinning.[10] —SN

Two hosts are needed for these common rusts.

Leaf spot is affecting my trees and shrubs. Is there a way to treat it?

There seems to be a leaf spot for every plant. I say that jokingly, but it's actually pretty close to the truth. Fortunately, they're usually easy to identify. They show up as speckles, blotches, or spots on the foliage of plants, and they can be coloured brown, black, yellow, red, orange, or purple. There are fungal and bacterial types, and some (mostly the bacterial ones) are much more serious than others. Proper sanitation is key to dealing with leaf spots. Clean up leaf and fruit litter. Do not water the foliage of plants; keep that stream of water from the garden hose at the base of the plants only. (I know, I know. There's nothing we can do about rain. We can only control what we're able to.) Prune out affected areas, and sterilize your pruning tools as you cut. Don't compost the trimmings or use them in any other way in the garden. Depending on the type of leaf spot, you may need to remove the plant altogether—they can be that fiendish. Your arborist will be extremely helpful in diagnosing and figuring out a treatment plan for affected plants.[11] — SN

My coniferous trees are infected with needle cast. Are there any ways to control it?

Needle cast is a serious fungal disease affecting conifers such as spruce. If you see sections of your tree turning yellow, then brown, and the needles are dropping like crazy, this may be the culprit. Meticulous sanitation is necessary to try to prevent needle cast. Try to sweep up as many dead needles as you can, and dispose of them (not in the compost!). Do this as soon as you see the needles fall—don't let them sit and then do the job all at once before the snow flies. You need to keep up with this task to prevent the fungus from spreading.

Needle cast tends to more readily affect trees suffering from stress-related problems, such as prolonged drought. Set up a regular watering schedule, if you don't already have one, and stick to it. Trees suffering from root girdling may also be more susceptible to needle cast. (See pages 61–62 for our tips on preventing girdling.)

If your tree is really densely branched, it may be necessary to judiciously prune to open up the canopy so air and sunlight can move more freely through the tree. This isn't something to take lightly with conifers such as spruce because a bad pruning job can make your tree unsightly, and you are also opening up wounds that can be potentially infected with pathogens. If you choose to go this route, sterilize your pruning tools after every cut, and, whatever you do, don't rip bark off or damage the branch collars. I recommend consulting with an arborist before making this decision, and having them do the work for you.[12]—SN

Deer are the bane of my garden's existence! How can I keep them from destroying my trees and shrubs?

There is no need to describe this graceful ungulate—although they may be beautiful, deer are the bane of gardeners across the prairies. Deer will consume pretty much anything that has leaves, and you are unfortunately mistaken if you think all those "deer-resistant" plant lists are going to give you any assistance. The only thing deer respect—besides natural predators such as coyotes, wolves, bobcats, and cougars—is a very tall fence (and I mean very tall—they can jump 8 feet or 2.4 metres or more!). Deer tend to do the most damage to trees and shrubs in the winter, when food is scarce, but they also love completely mowing down your newly planted saplings. They will eat twigs, branches, and bark. They can easily girdle trees and shrubs and cause major entrance wounds on tree trunks, which can lead to further problems down the road if pathogens enter the injured sites.

Honestly, appropriate fencing and a big dog or two regularly patrolling your yard are the only ways to deter deer. Scent-based products, such as those made from an odiferous combination of ingredients such as eggs, capsaicin, garlic, fish meal, and castor oil, may be effective, but most gardeners don't apply them in the winter. Metal cage-style tree guards can protect lower trunks from damage, but deer can reach higher than most guards.[13]—SN

Deer have stripped off an alarming amount of bark from this tree.

I have a porcupine in my yard. Is there any way to deter it from gnawing on my trees and shrubs?

These large, quilled rodents are particularly skilled at stripping bark and trimming twigs, and the damage is most evident after a long, cold winter (although they will also seize the opportunity at other times of the year). Like deer, porcupines can girdle a tree if they remove enough bark and gnaw deeply enough into the tissues underneath. Porcupines are adept at climbing and have a reach that other critters can't manage. Mesh tree guards simply serve as ladders for them. You can install metal flashing material to a height of at least thirty inches (seventy-six centimetres) from the base of the tree. They cannot climb the slippery-smooth surface. Some gardeners have found that repellents containing the bitter compound thiram keep porcupines out of their gardens (but, of course, you cannot apply this product to edible plants).[14]—SN

My trees have been seriously damaged by voles. Is there something that can be done about these pesky rodents?

Resembling large, long mice with short tails (indeed, their common name is meadow or field mice), voles are seldom seen unless your cat brings you a dead one as a gift. Chances are, however, that come spring, you've observed in dismay and horror the winding tunnels voles make on a lawn beneath the winter snow, or you've seen evidence of substantial gnawing at the bases of young trees. For their size, voles can do quite a bit of damage to a newly planted tree while the world is buried in snow. While tree guards are not particularly effective against deer, they are perfect to thwart voles. Sink the guards into the ground—at least 3 inches (7.6 centimetres) below the soil surface. (This preventive method also works against rabbits!)

When you do your annual fall cleanup, crop the lawn short. Clean up leaf litter. The key is to remove places voles can hide in. And remember, once the tree has a few years under its belt, it is usually less desirable for voles to eat.[15] —SN

Set up a tree guard to protect your young trees against critters such as voles and rabbits.

Woodpeckers are drilling holes in my trees! How can I stop them?

Woodpeckers can make a serious impact (pun intended!) on a tree as they search out insects and grubs below the surface of the bark. Sapsucker damage is particularly notable as it looks like rows of precision-drilled oblong cavities in the bark. Once you've seen it, you'll never mistake it for anything else again.

Most woodpecker species don't attack healthy trees. Healthy trees don't have insects residing in their trunks. So, if you are seeing woodpecker damage, you're likely looking at a tree on its last legs.

Sapsuckers, which are a type of woodpecker, are an exception. They attack living, thriving trees because they want to dine on the sap inside the trees. Trees that are not severely damaged will usually make a full recovery on their own, but it is not unusual for the birds to girdle the plants. Deter them by hanging noisemakers and objects that flash in the branches of trees, which may startle the birds.

If the damage has been done by another species of woodpecker, consult with an arborist to ensure the attacked tree isn't so creaky that it will fall down in a storm and damage something or someone. If it is acceptable to leave it in place for a while longer, let the woodpeckers enjoy their meals and have fun watching them. They are remarkable, beautiful birds. Woodpeckers in Canada are a protected species under the Migratory Birds Convention Act, which means you cannot legally harm them. So although it is sad to see your tree perish, respect the process as part of the cycle of life.[16] —SN

Sapsuckers drill easily identifiable patterns of holes in the trunks of trees. (Photo courtesy of Gail Kozun Bruckner)

Why are squirrels ripping the bark off my trees?

Squirrels are created to annoy gardeners. They dig in containers, bury nuts in garden beds, and dig up spring bulbs. They also love stripping bark from our thin-skinned trees, such as aspen, birch, Amur cherry, and Russian olive, along with shrubs such as honeysuckle and ninebark.

Gardeners see this behaviour at the tail end of winter and the beginning of spring. The chewed-off bark is used to line the squirrels' nests for the new arrivals to come. The exposed cambium layer contains sugars and other needed nutrients when there is little else for squirrels to eat. This activity also keeps their teeth sharp. They use twigs for the same purpose, too.

A win-win-win for the squirrels, but not so much for the trees as the exposed cambium is vulnerable to pathogens and makes it easier for insects to get into the trees. Too much bark removal may also result in the death of branches or stems or, potentially, the whole plant.

Creating a guard to protect the trunk or limb will help deter them, but there isn't too much you can do to discourage them and prevent twigs from raining down on you as you work in your garden. Some suggest feeding the squirrels so they leave your trees alone. Others go for a repellent containing capsaicin. Me, I have three cats, and they are always on guard!

In any event, be on the lookout for this squirrel behaviour, and always monitor the health of your trees.[17] —**JM**

Squirrels can do a lot of damage to trees and shrubs. Good thing they are cute! (Photo courtesy of Tina Boisvert)

Trees and Shrubs for
All Occasions

5

Which trees and shrubs have the most show-stopping flower displays? Which ones have fragrant flowers?

Conspicuous flowers are a feature many gardeners look for in both ornamental and edible trees and shrubs, and some also enjoy those plants that are highly scented as well. (I suppose some gardeners actually *don't* want fragrance or a huge floral display—in which case, they should avoid this list!) An asterisk (*) following the names of the plants below indicates cultivars that are fragrant—but bear in mind that in some species (roses, for example), not all are scented.

* Apple and crabapple (*Malus* spp.)*
* Dogwood (*Cornus* spp.)
* *Forsythia* spp.
* Golden currant (*Ribes aureum*)*
* Hawthorn (*Crataegus* spp.)*
* Honey locust (*Gleditsia triacanthos*)*
* Honeysuckle (*Lonicera* spp.)*
* *Hydrangea* spp.*
* Lilac (*Syringa* spp.)*
* Linden (*Tilia* spp.)*
* Lydia broom (*Genista lydia*)
* Mock orange (*Philadelphus* spp.)*
* Mountain ash (*Sorbus* spp.)
* Ninebark (*Physocarpus* spp.)
* Potentilla (*Potentilla reptans*)
* *Prunus* spp. (especially mayday, chokecherry, flowering almond, pin cherry, sand cherry, plum)*
* *Rhododendron* spp.
* Saskatoon (*Amelanchier* spp.)
* *Spiraea* spp.
* Ussurian pear (*Pyrus ussuriensis*)
* *Viburnum* spp. (especially *V. opulus*)
* *Weigela* spp.—SN

Yes, mock orange flowers really do smell like orange blossoms!

Most gardeners think of lindens as massive shade trees, but they also happen to sport these adorable and lightly scented flowers in early summer.

Which trees and shrubs have the most striking autumn leaf colour?

The aesthetic value of trees and shrubs extends to growth habit, the texture and shape of the leaves, the colour and showiness of the flowers, the beauty of the fruit and seed pods, and the colour and texture of the bark or the stems. For many gardeners, the desire quotient is significantly increased if the tree or shrub has glorious autumn foliage colour. While prairie gardeners can't grow some of the trees and shrubs that hold such "leaf peeper" appeal in the eastern parts of the country, we still have some pretty marvellous specimens to choose from.

RED OR ORANGE

* Autumn Magic black chokeberry (*Aronia melanocarpa* 'Autumn Magic')
* Burning bush (*Euonymus alatus*), especially Turkestan burning bush (*E. nana* 'Turkestanica')
* *Cotoneaster* spp.
* Maple (*Acer*)
    * Autumn Blaze maple (*A.* × *freemanii* 'Jeffersred')
    * Inferno sugar maple (*A. saccharum* 'Jeferno')
    * Rocky Mountain or Douglas maple (*A. glabrum*)
    * Tatarian maple (*Acer tataricum*)
* Mountain ash (*Sorbus* spp.)
* Oak (*Quercus*)
    * Bur oak (*Q. macrocarpa*)
    * Northern pin oak (*Q. ellipsoidalis*)
    * Northern red oak (*Q. rubra*)
* Ohio buckeye (*Aesculus glabra*)
* Saskatoon (*Amelanchier* spp., particularly 'Autumn Brilliance')
* Smooth sumac (*Rhus glabra*)
* Ussurian pear (*Pyrus ussuriensis*)
* *Viburnum* spp.
    * Nannyberry (*V. lentago*)
    * Snowball viburnum (*V. opulus*)

YELLOW

* Amur cherry (*Prunus maackii*)
* Amur cork (*Phellodendron amurense*)
* Beaked hazelnut (*Corylus cornuta*)
* Hawthorn (*Crataegus* × *mordenensis* 'Snowbird' and 'Toba')
* Larch (*Larix* spp.)
* Mancana Manchurian ash (*Fraxinus mandshurica* 'Mancana')
* Poplar (*Populus* spp.)
* Silver Cloud silver maple (*Acer saccharinum* 'Silver Cloud')[1] — SN

Larches are deciduous conifers that have spectacular colour in autumn (until all the needles fall off, that is!).

Which trees and shrubs have beautiful bark and stem texture and colour?

In a country where our deciduous trees and shrubs are without leaves for a good part of the year, their bark becomes a most important feature. In winter our eyes are drawn to the twigs and trunks of our woodies, and they dazzle our eyes against the twinkly snow and lend texture to a muted world.

Thankfully, we are not lacking in lovely trees and shrubs with both characteristics. Here are some to consider:

TREES

* American elm (*Ulmus americana*): Thick, dark grey, and deeply furrowed bark
* Birch (*Betula*)
    * Paper birch (*B. papyrifera*): An iconic tree with white bark that peels off in strips
    * River birch (*B. nigra*): Peeling, multicoloured bark from tan to salmon and cream
* Bur oak (*Quercus macrocarpa*): Corky, ridged bark
* Cherry (*Prunus*)
    * Amur cherry (*P. maackii*): Shiny, peeling copper bark with wide white lenticels
    * Pin cherry (*P. pensylvanica*): Reddish-brown bark with wide lenticels
* Japanese tree lilac (*Syringa reticulata*) and cultivar 'Ivory Silk': Deep brown with wide, white lenticels
* Mountain ash (*Sorbus* spp.): Smooth, shiny bark in various colours
* Rocky Mountain Douglas fir (*Pseudotsuga menziesii* var. *glauca*): Thick, deeply furrowed reddish-brown bark
* Scot's pine (*Pinus sylvestris*): Papery, peeling orange bark
* Snowbird or Toba hawthorn (*Crataegus* × *mordenensis* 'Snowbird' or 'Toba'): Mature trees possess twisting trunks with deep grey ridges

* Trembling aspen (*Populus tremuloides*): Smooth greenish-white bark

SHRUBS

* Dogwood (*Cornus* spp.): Renowned for their red, yellow, or maroon stems, depending on the species
* Common ninebark (*Physocarpus opulifolius*) and various cultivars: Well-named with layers of peeling, shredding bark from tan to cream
* Harry Lauder's walking stick (*Corylus avellana* 'Contorta'): Bizarrely twisting stems
* Prickly rose (*Rosa acicularis*): Reddish and thickly covered with spines
* Purple osier willow (*Salix purpurea* 'Gracilis'): Slender, purplish stems
* Sutherland caragana (*Caragana arborescens* 'Sutherland'): Shiny olive-green/copper bark[2] —JM

Amur cherry trees have exceptional bark colour. The white lenticels against a coppery background are striking all year round.

What are some good compact trees for my small yard?

This list is by no means comprehensive—there are more and more compact trees being bred and becoming available to home gardeners every year. If you need a tree with a narrow form, look for the words "columnar" or "pyramidal" in the plant description. Otherwise, carefully check plant labels for mature height and spread.

DECIDUOUS TREES

* Birch (*Betula*)
  * Dakota Pinnacle birch (*B. platyphylla* 'Fargo')
  * Parkland Pillar birch (*B. platyphylla* 'Jefpark')
  * Young's weeping birch (*B. platyphylla* 'Youngii')
* Crabapple (*Malus*)
  * Emerald Spire flowering crabapple (*M.* × 'Jefgreen', 'Emerald Spire')
  * Purple Spire flowering crabapple (*M.* × 'Jefspire', 'Purple Spire')
  * Rosthern flowering crabapple (*M.* × 'Rosthern')
* Lilac (*Syringa*)
  * Dwarf Korean lilac (top grafted) (*S. meyeri* 'Palibin' TG)
  * Ivory Silk lilac (*S. reticulata* 'Ivory Silk')
  * Miss Kim lilac (top grafted) (*S. patula* 'Miss Kim' TG)
* Mountain ash (*Sorbus*)
  * Luxor pyramidal mountain ash (*S. aucuparia* 'Fastigiata')
  * Red Cascade mountain ash (*S. americana* 'Red Cascade')
* Oak (*Quercus*)
  * Regal Prince oak (*Q.* × *warei* 'Regal Prince')
* Plum (*Prunus*)
  * Muckle plum (*P.* × *nigrella* 'Muckle')
  * Princess Kay plum (*P. nigra* 'Princess Kay')

An Ivory Silk lilac is a beautiful ornamental selection for small yards. It also blooms a bit later in the summer than other lilac varieties.

This diminutive globe spruce (Picea pungens 'Globosa') on a standard is ideal for a small-space garden and is a real conversation starter!

CONIFERS

* Fir (*Abies*) and juniper (*Juniperus*) and pine (*Pinus*)
    * Dwarf balsam fir (*A. balsamea* 'Nana')
    * Upright junipers (*J. scopulorum* 'Cologreen', 'Medora', 'Moonglow', and 'Wichita Blue')
    * Columnar white pine (*P. strobus* 'Fastigiata')
* Spruce (*Picea*)
    * Columnar blue spruce (*P. pungens* 'Fastigiata')
    * Columnar Norway spruce (*P. abies* 'Cupressina')
    * Globe spruce (*P. pungens* 'Globosa' tree form)
    * Montgomery blue spruce (*P. pungens* 'Montgomery')
    * Weeping Norway spruce (*P. abies* 'Pendula')
    * Weeping white spruce (*P. glauca* 'Pendula')[3] —SN

Cotoneasters are one of the most common shrubs you'll find in urban settings on the prairies. They are not usually grown for their flowers, which are tiny (but delicate and pretty). If you want to grow cotoneasters, try them with other suitable selections in a mixed hedge so you minimize the risk of disease and pests wiping out all of your plants.

What are the top choices for shrubs to use as hedging?

The prairies have fewer options for hedges than many other biomes. Not for us are the formal yew hedges of the United Kingdom or even dense walls of cedar, at least not easily or without heartache if we have a winter that really tests the hardiness of our plants!

As a result, Peking cotoneaster (*Cotoneaster acutifolia*) and hedge cotoneaster (*C. lucidus*) are ubiquitous in modern urban landscapes on the prairies. They are almost a monoculture, accompanied by all the pest problems a monoculture brings. In older neighbourhoods and rural areas common caragana (*Caragana arborescens*) is also dominant, planted for its nitrogen-fixing attributes and extreme hardiness, but oh so prolific in self-sowing babies.

But there are other choices for hedging and high and low privacy screening, some more informal in nature than others. Here are some to consider:

* Alpine currant (*Ribes alpinum*)
* Boxwood (*Buxus* 'Calgary' or 'Green Velvet')
* Burning bush (*Euonymus alatus*)
* Cedar (*Thuja*)
    * Skybound cedar (*T. occidentalis* 'Skybound')
    * Wareana cedar (*T. occidentalis* 'Wareana')
* Cherry prinsepia (*Prinsepia sinensis*)
* Highbush cranberry (*Viburnum trilobum*), especially 'Bailey Compact'
* Japanese barberry (*Berberis thunbergii*)
* Lilac (*Syringa*)
    * Common lilac (*S. vulgaris*) and hybrids
    * Dwarf Korean lilac (*S. meyeri* 'Palibin' TG)
* Mugo pine (*Pinus mugo*)
* Northern Gold forsythia (*Forsythia* × *intermedia* 'Northern Gold')
* Saskatoon (*Amelanchier alnifolia*) and cultivars (native plant)
* Sutherland caragana (*Caragana arborescens* 'Sutherland')
* Willow (*Salix* spp.)[4] —JM

I'm looking for the best ground cover shrubs for my garden. What are some good selections?

Horizontal, mounding, or weeping shrubs add a lot of variety to any garden. As with all ground cover plants, they serve as living mulch and convey all the benefits from mulching, including conserving soil moisture, moderating soil temperature, helping to control soil erosion and weeds, and providing habitat for wildlife.

Consider these ground cover plants for your garden:

* Bearberry or kinnikinnick (*Arctostaphylos uva-ursi*)
* Bunchberry (*Cornus canadensis*)
* Creeping cotoneaster (*Cotoneaster adpressus*)
* Hillside Creeper pine (*Pinus sylvestris* 'Hillside Creeper')
* Juniper (*Juniperus*)
    * Common juniper (*J. communis*)
    * Creeping juniper (*J. horizontalis*)
* Lydia broom or woadwaxen (*Genista lydia*)
* Siberian cypress (*Microbiota decussata*)
* Spruce (*Picea*)
    * Bird's nest spruce (*P. abies* 'Nidiformis')
    * Prostrate Norway spruce (*P. abies* 'Prostrata')
* Weigela (*Weigela* spp.)
* Winter creeper euonymus (*Euonymus fortunei*)[5] —JM

My cedar (arborvitae) trees are drying out and dying. What other types of conifers can I plant as a substitute?

Cedars are valued for their upright shape and dense foliage, used as stand-alone specimens, foundation plantings, and hedging. Yet they have a well-deserved reputation for being tricky to establish on the prairies with our more severe winters, drying winds, and heavier soils. Once established, though, they can survive and thrive for years.

All is not lost, as there are several options to consider for prairie gardens:

* Juniper (*Juniperus*)
    * Blue Arrow juniper (*J. scopulorum* 'Blue Arrow')
    * Chinese juniper (*J. chinensis*)
    * Cologreen juniper (*J. scopulorum* 'Cologreen')
    * Common juniper (*J. communis*)
    * Dwarf pencil point juniper (*J. communis* 'Compressa')
    * Eastern red cedar (*J. virginiana*)
    * Mint Julep juniper (*J. chinensis* 'Mint Julep')
    * Medora juniper (*J. scopulorum* 'Medora')
    * Moonglow juniper (*J. scopulorum* 'Moonglow')
    * Rocky Mountain juniper (*J. scopulorum*) has many reliable cultivars, including 'Sky Rocket' and 'Wichita Blue'
* Pine (*Pinus*)
    * Chalet Swiss stone pine (*P. cembra* 'Chalet')
    * Columnar eastern white pine (*P. strobus* 'Fastigiata')
    * Columnar mugo pine (*P. mugo* 'Columnaris')
    * Columnar Scot's pine (*P. sylvestris* 'Fastigiata')
    * Eastern white pine (*P. strobus*)
    * Green Penguin dwarf Scot's pine (*P. sylvestris* 'Green Penguin')
    * Mugo pine (*P. mugo*)
    * Scot's pine (*P. sylvestris*)
    * Silver Whispers Swiss stone pine (*P. cembra* 'Silver Whispers')
    * Tip Top Swiss stone pine (*P. cembra* 'Tip Top')

✳ Spruce (*Picea*)

    ✳ Blue spruce (*P. pungens*)

    ✳ Blue Wonder dwarf Alberta spruce (*P. glauca* 'Blue Wonder')

    ✳ Columnar blue spruce (*P. pungens* 'Fastigiata')

    ✳ Dwarf Serbian spruce (*Picea omorika* 'Nana')

    ✳ North Star dwarf white spruce (*P. glauca* 'North Star')

    ✳ White spruce (*P. glauca*)[6]—JM

On the prairies, it's difficult to maintain cedar trees to the standard of excellence shown here. Fortunately, there are many other substitutes to choose from.

What are some good tree and shrub selections for dry sites?

One thing to remember when planting trees and shrubs (or any plant, really!) with low water requirements is they usually don't arrive at their drought-tolerant status until their roots are well-established, which can take time—up to a year or more. As well, even though these selections are suitable for dry sites, they will still periodically require water, and supplemental irrigation is a must when prolonged heat and drought conditions dictate. But, if you need a tree or shrub that can handle being a bit thirsty, here are some go-tos:

* Ash (*Fraxinus* spp.)
* Honeysuckle (*Lonicera* spp.)
* Juniper (*Juniperus* spp.)
* Ohio buckeye (*Aesculus glabra*)
* Pin cherry (*Prunus pensylvanica*)
* Potentilla (*Potentilla* spp.)[7]—SN

Honeysuckles are a pretty and practical selection for a dry garden.

What are some great tree and shrub selections for damp areas of the yard?

The following trees and shrubs will tolerate those spots in your garden where moisture dissipates slowly due to issues such as heavy soil or minor drainage issues brought on by sloping or uneven ground. What these plants won't do, however, is live in constantly boggy conditions. Soil that is saturated with water all the time chokes out the oxygen plant roots require, and the result is rot and death.

* Alder (*Alnus* spp.)
* Chokeberry (*Aronia* spp.)
* Elderberry (*Sambucus* spp.)
* Green ash (*Fraxinus pennsylvanica*)
* Hackberry (*Celtis occidentalis*)
* Red osier dogwood (*Cornus sericea*)
* River birch (*Betula nigra*)
* *Viburnum* spp.
* Willow (*Salix* spp.), including laurel leaf willow (*Salix pentandra*)[8] — SN

Viburnum opulus is a good choice for a damp site.

What are some fast-growing tree cultivars for the prairies?

While some tree species are genetically geared to grow faster, other factors will affect how quickly any species will grow. Access to water, sunlight, and nutrients will make a huge difference to growth rates, as will soil conditions and how well the tree was originally planted. Environmental constraints such as the length of the growing season, adverse winds, and extreme events such as drought, flooding, and the early onset of winter will also impact yearly growth.

Typically, softwood trees grow faster than hardwood trees because their wood is so much less dense. So, with all that in mind, here are a few species and cultivars to consider:

* American elm (*Ulmus americana*)
* Birch, especially paper (*Betula papyrifera*) and river (*B. nigra*)
* Columnar aspen, especially Swedish (*Populus tremula* 'Erecta') and tower (*Populus* × *canescens* 'Tower')
* Lodgepole pine (*Pinus contorta* var. *latifolia*)
* Manitoba maple (*Acer negundo*)
* Norway maple (*Acer platanoides*)
* Norway spruce (*Picea abies*) and many cultivars
* Poplar, any species or cultivar, but check out Prairie Sky poplar (*Populus* × *canadensis* 'Prairie Sky')
* Siberian larch (*Larix sibirica*)
* Willow, including laurel leaf (*Salix pentandra*) and golden (*Salix alba* var. *vitellina*)[9] —JM

What are the best tree and shrub selections for part shade?

Shade is difficult for most trees and shrubs, especially those that flower. They want and need to have as much sun as they can, and most placed in shadier conditions than their native habitat may survive but not thrive.

When choosing woody plants for shade, think about what you see in the wild. Beneath the shade cast by the dominant canopy are a few shrubs but mostly herbaceous plants.

That said, there are some choices for part shade that prefer cooler and not-so-bright conditions:

* Alpine currant (*Ribes alpinum*)
* Azalea, 'Northern Lights' series (*Rhododendron* spp.)
* Boxwood (*Buxus sinica* var. *insularis*)
* Daphne, rose (*Daphne cneorum*) and Carol Mackie (*Daphne × burkwoodii* 'Carol Mackie')
* Eastern hemlock (*Tsuga canadensis*)
* Hydrangea, paniculata or Peegee (*Hydrangea paniculata*) species and cultivars

Yew will perform nicely in sites located in part shade.

* Hydrangea, smooth (*Hydrangea arborescens*) cultivars, with 'Annabelle' the standard
* PJM Group rhododendron (*Rhododendron* 'PJM Elite')
* Saskatoon (*Amelanchier alnifolia*) and cultivars
* Snowberry (*Symphoricarpos* spp.)
* Sumac, Tiger Eyes (*Rhus typhina* 'Bailtiger')
* Viburnum (*Viburnum* spp.), a genus that includes highbush cranberry, nannyberry, and arrowwood
* Western mountain ash (*Sorbus scopulina*)
* Yew (*Taxus* spp.)

You will notice dogwood (*Cornus* spp.) is not listed, even though it is often sold as a shade shrub. It prefers wet feet, which is why it is usually considered a shade plant, but it actually thrives in full sun.

One more thing to keep in mind: many shrubs for the shade are poisonous! Be careful where children, pets, and wildlife are likely to be present.[10] —JM

Saskatoons are capable of handling part shade,
although they yield more berries if sited in full sun.

What are some amazing large trees that can fill my massive yard and provide lots of cooling shade and aesthetic value?

Large trees are focal points in any garden and deserve to be chosen with care for the many benefits they provide. Shade trees are valued for the cooling they offer, not only for the people sheltering underneath on a hot day but also for the cooling effect on nearby buildings. Here are some trees to consider:

* Brandon elm (*Ulmus americana* 'Brandon'): Grows up to fifty feet (fifteen metres) tall and close to thirty feet (ten metres) wide at the top.
* Bur oak (*Quercus macrocarpa*): Grows up to one hundred feet (thirty metres) tall and just as wide.
* Cutleaf weeping birch (*Betula pendula* 'Laciniata'): Grows up to forty feet (twelve metres) tall and twenty feet (six metres) wide.
* Dropmore linden (*Tilia × flavescens* 'Dropmore'): Grows up to forty feet (twelve metres) tall and twenty-plus feet (five to seven metres) wide.
* Green ash (*Fraxinus pennsylvanica*) and cultivars: Quick growing, but late leafing out and the first to lose their leaves. Make sure to choose a male cultivar, such as 'Patmore', to avoid prolific self-sowing.
* Laurel leaf willow (*Salix pentandra*): Grows up to forty feet (twelve metres) tall and just as broad.
* Mayday (*Prunus padus*): Grows up to thirty-plus feet (eleven metres) tall and twenty-five feet (eight metres) wide.
* Northern hackberry (*Celtis occidentalis*): Grows up to eighty feet (twenty-five metres) tall and twenty-five feet (eight metres) wide.
* Russian olive (*Elaeagnus angustifolia*): Unique species with airy, silver leaves that will grow up to thirty feet (nine metres) tall and twenty feet (six metres) wide on the prairies. This plant has a propensity to sucker, so site it appropriately.
* Silver Cloud silver maple (*Acer saccharinum* 'Silver Cloud'): Grows up to fifty feet (fifteen metres) tall and thirty feet (nine metres) wide.[11] —JM

What are some good tree and shrub selections for shelterbelts?

If you live in a rural setting on the prairies, wind can be a huge influence on your landscape. Planting a shelterbelt to control wind currents is necessary for so many reasons. For your garden, it means protection from the harsh elements that can desiccate and cause breakage to your plants. Shelterbelts can also prevent soil erosion and create a microclimate that may increase your chances of a successful harvest. As a homeowner, shelterbelts can reduce energy costs (particularly during extreme heat in the summer or the frigid equivalent in the winter) by decreasing the need for consumption. A shelterbelt might just save your home and outbuildings from losing shingles and becoming otherwise damaged during storms.

Your shelterbelt should be situated perpendicular to prevailing winds (on the prairies in the winter, the winds are usually from the north and the northwest). There is a formula for the zone a shelterbelt can protect, which should help you in selecting trees for your belt: multiply the height of the trees you have planted by seven. That number is how many metres the shelterbelt effectively protects. Remember you want to plant your shelterbelt at least a hundred feet (thirty metres) away from your home or outbuildings. (This is important when it comes to blowing, drifting snow!) Before you dig those planting holes, however, be sure you've checked with county regulations to ensure what the recommended allowances are—it may vary depending on where you live.

If you are planting your shelterbelt to deal more with hot, dry summer winds than with winter ones, your shelterbelt should be situated on the south and west sides of the area you wish to protect.

Multi-row shelterbelts are ideal, as they allow for the proper density to deal with wind velocity. Leave approximately twenty feet (six metres) of space between rows of trees.

Try a combination of these trees and shrubs in your shelterbelt:

* Bur oak (*Quercus macrocarpa*)
* Cherry (*Prunus*)
  * Chokecherry (*P. virginiana*)
  * Pin cherry (*P. pensylvanica*)
* Columnar aspen (*Populus tremula* 'Erecta')
* Green ash (*Fraxinus pennsylvanica*)
* Hawthorn (*Crataegus* spp.)
* Lilac (*Syringa* spp.)
* Red elderberry (*Sambucus racemosa*)
* Red osier dogwood (*Cornus sericea*)
* Saskatoon (*Amelanchier* spp.)
* Scot's pine (*Pinus sylvestris*)
* Siberian larch (*Larix sibirica*)
* Spruce (*Picea* spp.)[12] —SN

These columnar aspens perform double duty as shelterbelt plants and living privacy screens.

What are some fantastic wildlife- and bird-friendly trees and shrubs?

While some gardeners wouldn't dream of allowing—or, dare I say, *encouraging*—animals such as deer and squirrels to their gardens, others consciously want to tailor their landscapes so they provide sustenance, habitat, safety, and places for wildlife and birds to give birth and raise their young. If you fall within the second camp and want your garden to appeal to birds, squirrels, chipmunks, salamanders, frogs, bats, deer, rabbits, and other wonderful creatures, here is a list of trees and shrubs to plant:

* Balsam fir (*Abies balsamea*)
* Birch (*Betula* spp.)
* Butternut (*Juglans cinerea*)
* Chokecherry (*Prunus virginiana*)
* Crabapple and apple (*Malus* spp.)
* Dogwood (*Cornus* spp.)
* Hackberry (*Celtis occidentalis*)
* Hawthorn (*Crataegus* spp.)
* Lilac (*Syringa* spp.)
* Mountain ash (*Sorbus* spp.)
* Raspberry (*Rubus* spp.)
* Red elderberry (*Sambucus racemosa*)
* Saskatoon (*Amelanchier* spp.)
* Spruce (*Picea* spp.)
* *Viburnum* spp.[13]—SN

Dogwoods are great choices for a wildlife-friendly garden.

Celebrate all the benefits of trees and shrubs!

In Japan, there is a practice of *shinrin-yoku*, or forest bathing. Although the origin of the concept is hardly new, this specific type of therapeutic exercise was introduced in the 1980s to combat worker burnout and fatigue during the tech boom.[14] *Shinrin-yoku* has persisted and spread worldwide because spending time in nature is simply good for everyone! While many of us don't have a genuine forest in our backyards, we can still benefit from all that trees and shrubs provide for our gardens—and for us. So, go give those stalwarts of the prairie garden a grateful hug! (Maybe don't do it while the neighbours are watching, though.)—SN & JM

Acknowledgements

Janet and Sheryl would like to extend a massive thank you to the amazing, supportive, and talented publishing team at TouchWood Editions: Taryn Boyd and Tori Elliott (publisher and acting publisher), Kate Kennedy (editorial coordinator), Curtis Samuel (publicist and social media coordinator), Paula Marchese (copy editor), Meg Yamamoto (proofreader), Sydney Barnes (typesetter), and Pat Touchie (owner). A special thank you goes out to designer Tree Abraham, the creator of the gorgeous, unique cover art and all the beautiful trimmings for the books. We also want to give a shout-out to everyone behind the scenes: in distribution, in the warehouse, in the offices. The book you hold in your hands is a product of so much hard work from a lot of people!

We also want to extend heaps of gratitude to our fantastic readers who have given us such positive feedback about the books and told us to keep writing!

A special thank you as well to Tina Boisvert and Gail Kozun Bruckner, who generously contributed photography to the book, and to Steve Melrose, for providing us with our fantastic new author photos.

From Janet:

To my amazingly supportive family that provides all the encouragement I need to keep living my dream, despite my annoying habit of having my head in the clouds, thinking gardening even at the supper table! Special mention to the cats for providing chuckles with their funny personalities and demands for fuss-ups during all these most trying months with the pandemic raging.

To Sheryl—absolutely and totally bless the day you said, "Would you like to write a book with me?" An adventure, a deep dive into learning ever more about the evolving world of gardening, and a world of fun!

From Sheryl:

So much love to Rob and to my mum and dad and brother Derek—for everything, really and truly. I can't thank you enough. I also want to thank the rest of my family for their encouragement and support: all of my siblings-in-law, my nieces and nephews and the greats, as well as my aunts and uncles and cousins. I would name everyone, but we'd seriously run over the word count.

And heartfelt words for Janet: How fantastic is this? It is such a pleasure and so much fun to write these books together! I am so grateful!

Notes

Introduction

1. Weber et al., "Tree," Britannica (website).

2. Kolb, "What Makes a Tree Unique?," Extension Foundation (website).

3. Science Learning Hub (website), "What Is a Tree?"

Chapter One

1. Botts, "When Choosing a Tree or Shrub, Consider Its Mature Size and When You Will Plant It," *Chicago Tribune*; Jauron, "Factors to Consider When Selecting Trees and Shrubs," Iowa State University, Horticulture and Home Pest News; Love Your Landscape.org (website), "4 Things to Consider When Choosing Your Next Backyard Tree."

2. Tree Ottawa (website), "Planting a Caliper Tree"; Allen, "Tips for Choosing the Right Size Tree for Your Landscape," The Garden Continuum (website); Canadian Nursery Landscape Association, "Canadian Nursery Stock Standard, Ninth Edition."

3. City of Portland, Oregon, "How to Measure a Tree."

4. Botts, "In the Market for a New Tree? Bigger Isn't Better," *Chicago Tribune*; Sherwood's Forests (website), "Buying Trees: Big Trees Lead to a Skinny Wallet"; O'Connor, "What Size Tree Should I Plant?," Colorado State University Extension, Co-Horts blog; Reich, "Tree Planting 101 (Hint: It's Not What You've Heard)," Old House Online (website).

5. Chandler and Sheesley, "Multi-grafted Fruits Are a Practical Solution," Chron (website).

6. Iannotti, "Planting and Caring for Bare Root," The Spruce (website); BioAdvanced (website), "Growing Trees: Bare-Root Advantages and Timing"; Williamson, *Tree and Shrub Gardening for Alberta*, 29, 34–35; Bailey Nurseries (website), "Bareroot Planting Tips."

7. The Burlap Shop (website), "What Is Burlap?"; Williamson, *Tree and Shrub Gardening for Alberta*, 30, 35; Mattia, "Ball and Burlap Versus Potted Trees: What's the Difference?," Martha Stewart (website).

8. Gardener's Supply Company (website), "How to Plant a Tree or Shrub."

9. Lamp'l, "How to Plant a Tree the Right Way—7 Steps for Getting It Right Every Time," Growing a Greener World (website); Pavlis, "Planting Trees the Right Way," Garden Fundamentals (website); Williamson, *Tree and Shrub Gardening for Alberta*, 34.

10. Williamson, *Tree and Shrub Gardening for Alberta*, 38–39; Fountain, "Tree Care: The Planting Hole," University of Kentucky, College of Agriculture, Food and Environment; Ontario Ministry of Agriculture, Food and Rural Affairs, "Planting Habits."

11. Williamson, *Tree and Shrub Gardening for Alberta*, 39; Martin Jr. and Melby, *Home Landscapes, Planting, Design and Management*.

12. Pavlis, "Best Time to Plant Trees," Garden Myths (website); Lerner, "Fall Ideal for Planting Trees," Purdue University, Indiana Yard and Garden—Purdue Consumer Horticulture; Logan, "Why Don't Evergreens Change Color and Drop Their Leaves Every Fall?," The Conversation (website).

13. Williamson, *Tree and Shrub Gardening for Alberta*, 40–42.

Chapter Two

1. Jackson, "Mulching Landscape Trees," Purdue State Extension; Beaulieu, "Using Mulch around Trees," The Spruce (website).

2. Williamson, *Tree and Shrub Gardening for Alberta*, 46; Jackson, "Mulching Landscape Trees," Penn State Extension; Beaulieu, "Using Mulch around Trees," The Spruce (website); Trees.com (website), "Cedar Mulch in the Garden—Uses, Pros and Cons, and Problems"; Harris, "Is Landscape Fabric Ever Not Horrible?," Garden Rant (website).

3. Williams, *Creating the Prairie Xeriscape*, 45–52; Zuzek, "Watering Newly Planted Trees and Shrubs," University of Minnesota Extension; University of Minnesota Extension, "Watering Established Trees and Shrubs"; Adair Tree Care (website), "Watering Landscape Trees in Calgary."

4. Lonnee et al., *Growing Shrubs and Small Trees in Cold Climates*, 378–80; Day, "Protect Trees Now to Prevent Severe Winter Damage," Montana State University; Beaulieu, "How Often Should You Water Your Trees in the Fall?," The Spruce (website); Adair Tree Care (website), "Watering Trees in the Fall in Calgary"; Let's Talk Science (website), "How Do Trees Survive in Winter?"

5. Williamson, *Tree and Shrub Gardening for Alberta*, 48–49.

6. Chalker-Scott, "The Myth of Tree Topping," Plant Amnesty (website).

7. Landsman, "The ⅓ Rule for Pruning Shrubs," The Spruce (website); Haglund, "How to Prune: The Rules of Removal Percentages," Fiskars (website); Smith, "Basic Guidelines for Pruning Trees and Shrubs," North Dakota State University; Great Northern ReGreenery (website), "How Often Should You Prune Your Tree?"

8. Hemingway, "Rejuvenation Pruning: What, Why, When, and How," The Complete Pruning Guide (website); Carroll, "What Is Rejuvenation Pruning: Tips for Hard Pruning Plants," Gardening Know How (website); Harrison, "What Does Hard Pruning Mean?," PruningCuts.com (website); Espace Pour La Vie Montréal (website), "Pruning Deciduous Shrubs."

9. Landscape Ontario (website), "Pruning Shrubs and Evergreens."

10. Williamson, *Tree and Shrub Gardening for Alberta*, 50–52; Sproule, "Your Pruning Calendar," Salisbury Greenhouse (website); University of Manitoba, Faculty of Agriculture and Food Sciences, "Pruning Deciduous Ornamentals."

11. Government of Alberta, "Alberta's Elm Pruning Ban Starts April 1"; Trees Winnipeg (website), "Dutch Elm Disease"; Government of Saskatchewan, "Elm Tree Pruning Ban Begins April 1."

12. Graca, "Suberin: The Biopolyester at the Frontier of Plants," *Frontiers in Chemistry*.

13. Chalker-Scott, "The Myth of Wound Dressings," Wisconsin State University.

14. Carroll, "What Is Tree Wound Dressing: Is It Okay to Put Wound Dressing on Trees?," Gardening Know How (website); Harrison, "What Do You Put on a Tree after Cutting Off the Limb?," PruningCuts.com (website); Bradley, *The Pruner's Bible*, 24–25.

15. Missouri Botanical Garden (website), "Sunscald of Woody Plants"; SFGate (website), "What Type of Whitewash to Put on Fruit Trees?"; The Morton Arboretum (website), "Trunk Wounds and Decay."

16. Hole and Fallis, *Lois Hole's Favorite Trees and Shrubs*, 68; Skinner and Williams, *Best Trees and Shrubs for the Prairies*, 37.

17. Lipford, "How to Protect Trees and Shrubs from Cold Weather," Today's Homeowner (website); Scheufele et al., "Protecting Evergreens in the Winter Q&A," University of Massachusetts Amherst, Center for Agriculture, Food, and the Environment.

Chapter Three

1. Bloomfield, "Lilac Bush Is Not Blooming—Why Won't My Lilac Bush Bloom," Gardening Know How (website); Jauron, "Reasons Why Trees and Shrubs May Fail to Bloom," Iowa State University, Horticulture and Home Pest News.

2. Moore, "Ring-Barking and Girdling: How Much Vascular Connection Do You Need Between Roots and Crown?," TreeNet (website).

3. ArborCare (website), "Stump Grinding"; Hanrahan, "Wildlife Trees," Ottawa Field-Naturalists' Club (website).

4. Loewen, "Why Are My Brandon Cedars Turning Brown?," Fraser Valley Cedars (website); Grant, "Conifer Needles Turning Color: Why Does My Tree Have Discolored Needles," Gardening Know How (website); British Columbia Ministry of Agriculture, "Dying Cedar Hedges—What Is the Cause?"; Government of British Columbia, "Priority Conifer Pests and Pathogens."

5. Britannica (website), "Dieback"; University of Illinois Extension, "Decline and Dieback of Trees and Shrubs"; Davey (website), "How to Help Trees Recover from Winter Dieback."

6. Epcor (website), "Root Growth in Sewers"; City of Winnipeg, "Tree Roots"; The Morton Arboretum (website), "Tree Root Problems"; Carroll, "Invasive Tree Root List: Trees That Have Invasive Root Systems," Gardening Know How (website).

7. Knoll, "How to Remove Poplar Trees," Garden Guides (website); City of Calgary, "Problems with Poplar Trees."

8. Landsman, "Recognizing and Controlling Water Sprouts in Trees and Shrubs," The Spruce (website); Tree Weaver (website), "Epicormic Sprouts and Their Role in the Health of the Tree"; GraftinGardeners (website), "Tree Suckers and Water Sprouts (Epicormic Shoots)"; Virginia Cooperative Extension, "A Guide to Successful Pruning: Pruning Deciduous Trees."

9. Crassweller, "Home Orchards: Why Is There No Fruit on My Tree?," Penn State Extension; Patterson, "Apple Tree Problems—How to Get Fruit on Apple Trees," Gardening Know How (website).

10. Hirst, "Apple June Drop," Purdue University.

11. Crassweller, "Home Orchards: Why Is There No Fruit on My Tree?," Penn State Extension; Phys.org (website), "Northern Gardening Tips: When Fruit Trees Don't Bear Fruit, What's the Problem?"

12. Nix, "Leaf Abscission and Senescence," ThoughtCo. (website); Spengler, "Tree Leaves Didn't Drop in Winter: Reasons Why Leaves Did Not Fall Off a Tree," Gardening Know How (website).

13. Schill, "Why Are My Trees and Shrubs Not Leafing Out?," Schill Grounds Management (website); Patterson, "Deciduous Tree Leafing Problems: Why Won't My Tree Leaf Out?," Gardening Know How (website).

14. Stelzer, "First Aid for Storm-Damaged Trees," University of Missouri Extension; Glen, "Helping Trees and Shrubs Recover from Snow and Ice," Triangle Gardener (website).

Chapter Four

1. Sadof, "Landscape and Ornamentals: Scale Insects on Shade Trees and Shrubs," Purdue University Extension; Rosenthal, *Protect Your Garden*, 96–97.

2. Rosenthal, *Protect Your Garden*, 76–77; Williamson, *Tree and Shrub Gardening for Alberta*, 71.

3. Williamson, *Tree and Shrub Gardening for Alberta*, 69, 71; Rosenthal, *Protect Your Garden*, 73–75.

4. Albert, "Leafhoppers Natural Insect Pest Control," Harvest to Table (website).

5. City of Edmonton, "Sowbugs"; Government of Canada, "Centipedes, Millipedes, Sowbugs, and Pillbugs."

6. Valk, "Downy Mildew vs. Powdery Mildew," Greenhouse Canada (website).

7. Government of Alberta, "Black Knot."

8. Chalker-Scott, "Sterilized Pruning Tools: Nuisance or Necessity?," Washington State University Puyallup Research and Extension Center.

9. Williamson, *Tree and Shrub Gardening for Alberta*, 70.

10. Williamson, *Tree and Shrub Gardening for Alberta*, 73.

11. Planet Natural Research Center (website), "Leaf Spot."

12. Kanner and Grabowski, "Rhizosphaera Needle Cast," University of Minnesota Extension.

13. Perry, "Effective Deer Fences," University of Vermont, Department of Plant and Soil Sciences, The Green Mountain Gardener blog; Osborn and McConnell, "The Impact of Predators on Deer in the Southeast," University of Georgia, Warnell Outreach.

14. Government of Alberta, "Human-Wildlife Conflict—Porcupines."

15. City of Calgary, "Voles."

16. Government of Canada, "Yellow-Bellied Sapsucker."

17. SFGate (website), "Will a Squirrel Stripping the Bark off my Tree Kill the Tree?"; Squirrel Enthusiast (website), "Why Do Squirrels Eat Bark and What You Can Do about It."

Chapter Five

1. Sherwood's Forests (website), "Fall Colour: You Can Have Something Besides Yellow"; Tree Time (website), "Fall Colour Plants."

2. Knowles, *Woody Ornamentals for the Prairies*, 120, 130, 183, 202, 208, 215, 219; Williams, *Creating the Prairie Xeriscape*, 115, 121; Tree Canada (website), "Trees of Canada"; Williamson, *Tree and Shrub Gardening for Alberta*, 174–75, 224–25.

3. Sunstar Nurseries (website), "Deciduous Trees" and "Evergreens."

4. Hole and Fallis, *Lois Hole's Favorite Trees and Shrubs*, 26–27; Larum, "What Is Hedge Cotoneaster: Learn about Hedge Cotoneaster Care," Gardening Know How (website); LePage, "Top 5 Formal Hedges for Alberta," Wild Rose Garden & Tree Service (website); Sherwood's Forests (website), "Hedges: What Are They Good For?"

5. Williamson, *Tree and Shrub Gardening for Alberta*, 86–87, 135, 166–67; Carmolli, "Easy Care Landscaping with Low-Growing Ground Cover Shrubs," Proven Winners (website); Trees.com (website), "11 Best Evergreen Ground Cover Plants That Make Your Garden Look Greener and Better"; Wood, "No More Weeding or Mulching: Ground Covering Shrubs," The Plant Hunter (website).

6. Williamson, *Tree and Shrub Gardening for Alberta*, 193, 196–97, 236, 238; Krige, "Emerald Cedars: Not Always the Greenest Choice," CLC Tree Services (website); Caviness, "Upright Junipers vs. Arborvitae (Reviews)," Home Nursery Company (website); Landscape America (website), "Upright Junipers"; Walliser, "Dwarf Evergreen Trees: 15 Exceptional Choices for the Yard and Garden," Savvy Gardening (website); Mendonca, "Top Columnar Trees to Plant in Alberta," Sherwood Nurseries (website).

7. Ruzycki, "Drought-Tolerant Plants," *Edmonton Sun*; City of Edmonton, "Drought Resistant Trees, Shrubs and Perennials."

8. Landscape Ontario (website), "Gardening for Moist Areas"; Sellmer et al., "Trees, Shrubs, and Ground Covers Tolerant of Wet Sites," Penn State Extension.

9. Fratt, "How Do Some Trees Get So Big?," PlantSnap (website); Charlton & Jenrick (website), "Softwood vs. Hardwood"; Tree Time (website), "What Are the Best Fast Growing Trees in Alberta?"; Pevach (website), "Your Guide to Hardy, Fast Growing Trees in Alberta and Saskatchewan."

10. Williamson, *Tree and Shrub Gardening for Alberta*, 188–91, 250–53, 268–69, 274–75, 288–91, 294–99, 312–13; Myers, "29 Shrubs That Grow in Full or Partial Shade," The Spruce (website); Kohut, "Growing Azaleas in Manitoba Successfully," *Winnipeg Free Press*.

11. ArborCare (website), "Low-Maintenance Trees for Your Yard"; Sunstar Nurseries (website), "Deciduous Trees"; Tree Canada (website), "Northern Hackberry (*Celtis occidentalis*)"; Tree Time (website), "Common Hackberry vs. Prairie Sky Poplar."

12. Alberta Agriculture and Food, "Shelterbelts in Alberta."

13. Sherrill and Brittingham, "Landscaping for Wildlife: Trees, Shrubs, and Vines," Penn State Extension.

14. Fitzgerald, "The Secret to Mindful Travel? A Walk in the Woods," *National Geographic*.

Sources

Adair Tree Care (website). "Watering Landscape Trees in Calgary." Accessed May 12, 2021. adairtreecare.com/resources/insects-diseases/watering-landscape-trees-in-calgary.

———. "Watering Trees in the Fall in Calgary." Last updated September 15, 2011. adairtreecare.com/posts/watering-trees-in-the-fall-in-calgary.

Albert, Steve. "Leafhoppers Natural Insect Pest Control." Harvest to Table (website). Accessed September 24, 2021. harvesttotable.com/leafhoppers-natural-insect-pest -control/.

Alberta Agriculture and Food. "Shelterbelts in Alberta." 1992. open.alberta.ca /dataset/0c7aa2be-04b7-4cd3-a86f-7eb307219f41/resource/eee1ebcb-65ae-4b4f-9339 -2a73ef592f19/download/1992-277-20-2.pdf.

Allen, Monique. "Tips for Choosing the Right Size Tree for Your Landscape." The Garden Continuum (website). July 18, 2016. thegardencontinuum.com/blog/tips-for -choosing-the-right-size-tree-for-your-landscape.

ArborCare (website). "Low-Maintenance Trees for Your Yard." February 28, 2017. arborcare.com/blog/low-maintenance-trees-for-your-yard.

———. "Stump Grinding." Accessed May 15, 2021. arborcare.com/services/stump -grinding.

Bailey Nurseries (website). "Bareroot Planting Tips." Accessed May 12, 2021. baileynurseries.com/programs/bareroot/care/.

Beaulieu, David. "How Often Should You Water Your Trees in the Fall?" The Spruce (website). Last updated November 28, 2020. thespruce.com/when-should-i-be-watering -trees-in-fall-2130936.

———. "Using Mulch around Trees." The Spruce (website). Last updated September 2, 2018. thespruce.com/should-i-be-using-mulch-around-trees-2132626.

BioAdvanced (website). "Growing Trees: Bare-Root Advantages and Timing." Accessed May 12, 2021. bioadvanced.com/articles/growing-trees-bare-root-advantages-and-timing.

Bloomfield, Caroline. "Lilac Bush Is Not Blooming—Why Won't My Lilac Bush Bloom." Gardening Know How (website). Last updated December 3, 2020. gardeningknowhow.com/ornamental/shrubs/lilac/lilac-bush-not-blooming.htm.

Botts, Beth. "In the Market for a New Tree? Bigger Isn't Better." *Chicago Tribune*. July 5, 2017. chicagotribune.com/lifestyles/home-and-garden/ct-sun-0709-garden-morton -20170705-story.html.

———. "When Choosing a Tree or Shrub, Consider Its Mature Size and Where You Will Plant It." *Chicago Tribune*. September 10, 2018. chicagotribune.com/lifestyles /home-and-garden/ct-life-0916-garden-morton-20180910-story.html.

Bradley, Steve. *The Pruner's Bible: A Step-by-Step Guide to Pruning Every Plant in Your Garden*. Emmaus, PA: Rodale, 2005.

Britannica (website). "Dieback." July 20, 1998. britannica.com/science/dieback.

British Columbia Ministry of Agriculture. "Dying Cedar Hedges—What Is the Cause?" Last updated March 2015. www2.gov.bc.ca/assets/gov/farming-natural-resources-and -industry/agriculture-and-seafood/animal-and-crops/plant-health/dying-cedar-hedges.pdf.

Burlap Shop, The (website). "What Is Burlap?" Accessed May 12, 2021. theburlapshop .com/What-Is-Burlap.html#:~:text=Faux%20Burlap%20is%20made%20of,machine%20 washable%20and%20dyer%20safe.

Canadian Nursery Landscape Association. "Canadian Nursery Stock Standard, Ninth Edition." 2017. cnla.ca/uploads/pdf/Canadian-Nursery-Stock-Standard-9th-ed-web.pdf.

Carmolli, Natalie. "Easy Care Landscaping with Low-Growing Ground Cover Shrubs." Proven Winners (website). Accessed May 12, 2021. provenwinners.com/learn /finding-right-plant/easy-care-landscaping-low-growing-groundcover-shrubs.

Carroll, Jackie. "Invasive Tree Root List: Trees That Have Invasive Root Systems." Gardening Know How (website). Last updated April 3, 2021. gardeningknowhow.com /ornamental/trees/tgen/trees-with-invasive-roots.htm.

———. "What Is Rejuvenation Pruning: Tips for Hard Pruning Plants." Gardening Know How (website). Last updated July 2, 2021. gardeningknowhow.com/ornamental /shrubs/shgen/rejuvenation-pruning-tips.htm.

———. "What Is Tree Wound Dressing: Is It Okay to Put Wound Dressing on Trees?" Gardening Know How (website). Last updated January 5, 2021. gardeningknowhow .com/ornamental/trees/tgen/wound-dressing-on-trees.htm.

Caviness, Darlene. "Upright Junipers vs. Arborvitae (Reviews)." Home Nursery Company (website). November 9, 2012. homenursery.com/Blog-Post/Upright-Junipers -Vs-Arborvitae-Reviews.

Chalker-Scott, Linda. "The Myth of Tree Topping." Plant Amnesty (website). March 23, 2009. plantamnesty.org/wp-content/uploads/The-Myth-of-Tree-Topping.pdf.

———. "The Myth of Wound Dressings." Wisconsin State University. May 15, 2015. s3.wp.wsu.edu/uploads/sites/403/2015/03/wound-sealer.pdf.

———. "Sterilized Pruning Tools: Nuisance or Necessity?" Washington State University Puyallup Research and Extension Center. March 2015. s3.wp.wsu.edu /uploads/sites/403/2015/03/Pruning.pdf.

Chandler, Angela, and Heidi Sheesley. "Multi-grafted Fruits Are a Practical Solution." Chron (website). Last updated August 5, 2011. chron.com/life/gardening/article/Multi -grafted-fruits-are-a-practical-solution-1734991.php.

Charlton & Jenrick (website). "Softwood vs. Hardwood." Accessed May 12, 2021. charltonandjenrick.co.uk/news/2019/05/softwood-vs-hardwood/.

City of Calgary. "Problems with Poplar Trees." Accessed May 15, 2021. calgary.ca/csps /parks/planning-and-operations/tree-management/problems-with-poplar-trees.html.

———. "Voles." Accessed May 12, 2021. calgary.ca/csps/parks/planning-and -operations/pest-management/voles.html.

City of Edmonton. "Drought Resistant Trees, Shrubs and Perennials." Accessed May 12, 2021. edmonton.ca/residential_neighbourhoods/gardens_lawns_trees/drought -resistant-trees-shrubs.aspx.

———. "Sowbugs." Accessed May 11, 2021. edmonton.ca/programs_services/pests /sowbugs.aspx#:~:text=Sowbugs%20are%20a%20common%20sight,clothing%2C%20 or%20damage%20your%20home.

City of Portland, Oregon. "How to Measure a Tree." Accessed May 10, 2021. portland .gov/trees/tree-care-and-resources/how-measure-tree#:~:text=Diameter%20at%20 breast%20height%2C%20or,4.5%20feet%20above%20the%20ground.

City of Winnipeg. "Tree Roots." Last updated January 16, 2019. winnipeg.ca/finance /findata/riskmgt/tree_roots.stm.

Crassweller, Robert. "Home Orchards: Why Is There No Fruit on My Tree?" Penn State Extension. Last updated June 9, 2016. extension.psu.edu/home-orchards -why-is-there-no-fruit-on-my-tree.

Davey (website). "How to Help Trees Recover from Winter Dieback." March 19, 2020. blog.davey.com/2020/03/how-to-help-trees-recover-from-winter-dieback/.

Day, Toby. "Protect Trees Now to Prevent Severe Winter Damage." Montana State University. September 2, 2010. montana.edu/news/8747/protect-trees-now-to-prevent -severe-winter-damage.

Epcor (website). "Root Growth in Sewers." Accessed May 15, 2021. epcor.com/learn /about-our-drainage-system/repairs-damages/Pages/root-growth-in-sewers.aspx.

Espace Pour La Vie Montréal (website). "Pruning Deciduous Shrubs." Accessed May 13, 2021. espacepourlavie.ca/en/pruning-deciduous-shrubs.

Fitzgerald, Sunny. "The Secret to Mindful Travel? A Walk in the Woods." *National Geographic*. October 18, 2019. nationalgeographic.com/travel/article/forest-bathing -nature-walk-health.

Fountain, William M. "Tree Care: The Planting Hole." University of Kentucky, College of Agriculture, Food and Environment, Urban Forest Initiative. Accessed May 12, 2021. ufi.ca.uky.edu/treetalk/tree-planting-hole.

Fratt, Kayla. "How Do Some Trees Get So Big?" PlantSnap (website). October 19, 2018. plantsnap.com/blog/why-are-trees-tall/.

Gardener's Supply Company (website). "How to Plant a Tree or Shrub." Last updated July, 6 2021. gardeners.com/how-to/tree-planting/8741.html.

Glen, Charlotte. "Helping Trees and Shrubs Recover from Snow and Ice." Triangle Gardener (website). Accessed May 15, 2021. trianglegardener.com/helping-trees -and-shrubs-recover-from-snow-and-ice/#:~:text=Always%20sweep%20upward%20 %E2%80%93%20sweeping%20from,and%20shrubs%20to%20remove%20 snow.&text=Most%20shrubs%20damaged%20by%20snow,be%20severely%20 pruned%20if%20necessary.

Government of Alberta. "Alberta's Elm Pruning Ban Starts April 1." March 29, 2021. alberta.ca/albertas-elm-pruning-ban-starts-april-1.aspx.

———. "Black Knot." Accessed May 11, 2021. alberta.ca/black-knot.aspx.

———. "Human-Wildlife Conflict—Porcupines." Accessed May 12, 2021. alberta.ca /porcupines.aspx.

Government of British Columbia. "Priority Conifer Pests and Pathogens." Accessed May 15, 2021. www2.gov.bc.ca/gov/content/industry/forestry/managing-our-forest -resources/forest-health/forest-pests.

Government of Canada. "Centipedes, Millipedes, Sowbugs, and Pillbugs." Last updated June 4, 2013. canada.ca/en/health-canada/services/pest-control-tips/centipedes -millipedes-sowbugs-pillbugs.html.

———. "Yellow-Bellied Sapsucker." Last updated January 24, 2020. agriculture .canada.ca/en/agriculture-and-environment/agricultural-pest-management/diseases-and -pests/yellow-bellied-sapsucker.

Government of Saskatchewan. "Elm Tree Pruning Ban Begins April 1." March 25, 2019. saskatchewan.ca/government/news-and-media/2019/march/25/elm-tree-pruning-ban.

Graca, José. "Suberin: The Biopolyester at the Frontier of Plants." *Frontiers in Chemistry*. October 30, 2015. ncbi.nlm.nih.gov/pmc/articles/PMC4626755/.

GraftinGardeners (website). "Tree Suckers and Water Sprouts (Epicormic Shoots)." December 13, 2018. graftingardeners.co.uk/tree-suckers-water-sprouts/.

Grant, Amy. "Conifer Needles Turning Color: Why Does My Tree Have Discolored Needles." Gardening Know How (website). Last updated March 4, 2021. gardeningknowhow.com/ornamental/trees/tgen/brown-conifer-needles .htm#:~:text=Needles%20turning%20color%20may%20be,which%20results%20in%20 water%20loss.

Great Northern ReGreenery (website). "How Often Should You Prune Your Tree?" September 24, 2019. greatnorthernregreenery.com/how-often-should-you-prune-your-tree/.

Haglund, Robin. "How to Prune: The Rules of Removal Percentages." Fiskars (website). Accessed May 13, 2021. fiskars.com/en-us/gardening-and-yard-care/ideas-and -how-tos/pruning-and-trimming/how-to-prune-the-rules-of-removal-percentages.

Hanrahan, Christine. "Wildlife Trees." Ottawa Field-Naturalists' Club (website). Last updated July 1, 2012. ofnc.ca/programs/fletcher-wildlife-garden/make-your-own -wildlife-garden/wildlife-trees.

Harris, Susan. "Is Landscape Fabric Ever Not Horrible?" Garden Rant (website). December 22, 2017. gardenrant.com/2017/12/is-landscape-fabric-ever-not-horrible.html.

Harrison, Yates. "What Does Hard Pruning Mean?" PruningCuts.com (website). Accessed May 13, 2021. pruningcuts.com/what-does-hard-pruning-mean/.

———. "What Do You Put on a Tree after Cutting Off the Limb?" PruningCuts.com (website). Accessed May 15, 2021. pruningcuts.com/what-do-you-put-on-a-tree -after-cutting-off-the-limb/.

Hemingway, Monica. "Rejuvenation Pruning: What, Why, When, and How." The Complete Pruning Guide (website). February 1, 2015. pruningguide.com/rejuvenation -pruning/.

Hirst, Peter M. "Apple June Drop." Purdue University. May 27, 2016. fff.hort.purdue .edu/article/apple-june-drop/.

Hole, Lois, and Jill Fallis. *Lois Hole's Favorite Trees and Shrubs*. Tukwila, WA: Lone Pine Publishing, 1997.

Iannotti, Marie. "Planting and Caring for Bare Root." The Spruce (website). Last updated December 16, 2020. thespruce.com/bare-root-plants-1402450.

Jackson, David R. "Mulching Landscape Trees." Penn State Extension. Last updated April 12, 2018. extension.psu.edu/mulching-landscape-trees.

Jauron, Richard. "Factors to Consider When Selecting Trees and Shrubs." Iowa State University, Horticulture and Home Pest News. April 18, 2003. hortnews.extension .iastate.edu/2003/4-18-2003/treesandshrubs.html.

———. "Reasons Why Trees and Shrubs May Fail to Bloom." Iowa State University, Horticulture and Home Pest News. May 18, 1994. hortnews.extension.iastate .edu/1994/5-18-1994/nobloom.html.

Kanner, Cynthia Ash, and Michelle Grabowski. "Rhizosphaera Needle Cast." University of Minnesota Extension. 2019. extension.umn.edu/plant-diseases /rhizosphaera-needle-cast.

Knoll, Elizabeth. "How to Remove Poplar Trees." Garden Guides (website). September 21, 2017. gardenguides.com/93645-remove-poplar-trees.html.

Knowles, Hugh. *Woody Ornamentals for the Prairies*. Edmonton: University of Alberta, 1989.

Kohut, James. "Growing Azaleas in Manitoba Successfully." *Winnipeg Free Press*. August 24, 2013. homes.winnipegfreepress.com/winnipeg-real-estate-articles /renovation-design/Growing-Azaleas-In-Manitoba-successfully/id-3514.

Kolb, Peter. "What Makes a Tree Unique?" Extension Foundation (website). May 16, 2019. climate-woodlands.extension.org/what-makes-a-tree-unique/#:~:text=They%20 are%20also%20unique%20because,recorded%20tree%20is%20a%20giant.

Krige, Katherine. "Emerald Cedars: Not Always the Greenest Choice." CLC Tree Services (website). November 24, 2016. clctreeservices.com/emerald-cedars-not-greenest-choice/.

Lamp'l, Joe. "How to Plant a Tree the Right Way—7 Steps for Getting It Right Every Time." Growing a Greener World (website). April 18, 2017. growingagreenerworld .com/how-to-plant-a-tree/.

Landscape America (website). "Upright Junipers." Accessed May 12, 2021. landscape -america.com/landscapes/upright_junipers.html.

Landscape Ontario (website). "Gardening for Moist Areas." Accessed June 3, 2013. landscapeontario.com/gardening-for-moist-areas.

———. "Pruning Shrubs and Evergreens." May 29, 2013. landscapeontario .com/pruning-shrubs--evergreens#:~:text=Clip%20them%20with%20hedge%20 shears,the%20pruning%20will%20be%20unseen.

Landsman, Jonathan. "The ⅓ Rule for Pruning Shrubs." The Spruce (website). Last updated January 5, 2020. thespruce.com/pruning-rule-of-thirds-for-shrubs-3269526.

———. "Recognizing and Controlling Water Sprouts in Trees and Shrubs." The Spruce (website). Last updated March 22, 2021. thespruce.com/what-are-watersprouts-3269561.

Larum, Darcy. "What Is Hedge Cotoneaster: Learn about Hedge Cotoneaster Care." Gardening Know How (website). Last updated January 5, 2021. gardeningknowhow.com/ornamental/shrubs/cotoneaster/hedge-cotoneaster-care.htm.

LePage, Shane. "Top 5 Formal Hedges for Alberta." Wild Rose Garden & Tree Service (website). March 11, 2015. wildrosetree.ca/top-5-formal-hedges-for-alberta/.

Lerner, Rosie. "Fall Ideal for Planting Trees." Purdue University, Indiana Yard and Garden—Purdue Consumer Horticulture. Last updated March 27, 2006. purdue.edu/hla/sites/yardandgarden/fall-ideal-for-planting-trees/.

Let's Talk Science (website). "How Do Trees Survive in Winter?" March 16, 2020. letstalkscience.ca/educational-resources/stem-in-context/how-do-trees-survive-in-winter.

Lipford, Danny. "How to Protect Trees and Shrubs from Cold Weather." Today's Homeowner (website). Accessed May 15, 2021. todayshomeowner.com/how-to-protect-your-trees-and-shrubs-with-anti-desiccants/.

Loewen, Brandon. "Why Are My Brandon Cedars Turning Brown?" Fraser Valley Cedars (website). August 24, 2020. fraservalleycedars.com/why-are-my-brandon-cedars-turning-brown/#:~:text=Fungal%20disease%2C%20like%20root%20rot,or%20remove%20the%20affected%20areas.

Logan, Barry. "Why Don't Evergreens Change Color and Drop Their Leaves Every Fall?" The Conversation (website). October 21, 2019. theconversation.com/why-dont-evergreens-change-color-and-drop-their-leaves-every-fall-123744.

Lonnee, Debbie, Nancy Rose, Don Selinger, and John Whitman. *Growing Shrubs and Small Trees in Cold Climates*. Rev. ed. Minneapolis, MN: University of Minnesota Press, 2011.

Love Your Landscape.org (website). "4 Things to Consider When Choosing Your Next Backyard Tree." Accessed May 8, 2021. loveyourlandscape.org/expert-advice/tree-care/tree-selection/4-things-to-consider-when-choosing-your-next-backyard-tree/.

Martin, Edward C., Jr., and Pete Melby. *Home Landscapes, Planting, Design and Management*. Portland, OR: Timber Press, 1995. mrwa.org/wp-content/uploads/repository/const_tec_trees.pdf.

Mattia, Nancy. "Ball and Burlap Versus Potted Trees: What's the Difference?" Martha Stewart (website). May 14, 2019. marthastewart.com/1539451/ball-and-burlap-versus-potted-trees-explained.

Mendonca, Sarah. "Top Columnar Trees to Plant in Alberta." Sherwood Nurseries (website). July 4, 2019. sherwoodnurseries.ca/top-columnar-trees-to-plant-in-alberta/.

Missouri Botanical (website). "Sunscald of Woody Plants." Accessed January 7, 2021. missouribotanicalgarden.org/gardens-gardening/your-garden/help-for-the-home-gardener/advice-tips-resources/pests-and-problems/environmental/sunscald/sunscald-of-woody-plants.aspx.

Moore, G.M. "Ring-Barking and Girdling: How Much Vascular Connection Do You Need Between Roots and Crown?" TreeNet (website). 2013. treenet.org/resources/ring-barking-girdling-much-vascular-connection-need-roots-crown/.

Morton Arboretum, The (website). "Tree Root Problems." Accessed May 15, 2021. mortonarb.org/trees-plants/tree-and-plant-advice/horticulture-care/tree-root-problems.

———. "Trunk Wounds and Decay." Accessed January 9, 2021. mortonarb.org /trees-plants/tree-and-plant-advice/horticulture-care/trunk-wounds-and-decay #:~:text=If%20less%20than%2025%25%20of,tree%20paint)%20is%20not%20 necessary.

Myers, Vanessa Richins. "29 Shrubs That Grow in Full or Partial Shade." The Spruce (website). February 19, 2021. thespruce.com/shrubs-for-shade-areas-3269720.

Nix, Steve. "Leaf Abscission and Senescence." ThoughtCo. (website). Last updated January 8, 2020. thoughtco.com/leaf-abscission-and-senescence -1342629#:~:text=The%20word%20abscission%20in%20biological,various%20 parts%20of%20an%20organism.&text=Most%20deciduous%20(means%20 'falling',trees)%20continuously%20abscise%20their%20leaves.

O'Connor, Alison. "What Size Tree Should I Plant?" Colorado State University Extension, Co-Horts blog. October 27, 2016. csuhort.blogspot.com/2016/10/what -size-tree-should-i-plant.html.

Ontario Ministry of Agriculture, Food and Rural Affairs. "Planting Habits." Last updated February 12, 2021. omafra.gov.on.ca/english/crops/facts/plnthbts.htm.

Osborn, David A., and Mark D. McConnell. "The Impact of Predators on Deer in the Southeast." University of Georgia, Warnell Outreach. December 2016. warnell. uga.edu/sites/default/files/publications/WSFNR-16-51%20McConnell.pdf.

Patterson, Susan. "Apple Tree Problems—How to Get Fruit on Apple Trees." Gardening Know How (website). Last updated July 6, 2021. gardeningknowhow .com/edible/fruits/apples/no-fruit-on-apple-trees.htm.

———. "Deciduous Tree Leafing Problems: Why Won't My Tree Leaf Out?" Gardening Know How (website). Last updated June 18, 2021. gardeningknowhow .com/ornamental/trees/tgen/tree-leafing-problems.htm.

Pavlis, Robert. "Best Time to Plant Trees." Garden Myths (website). Last updated December 2018. gardenmyths.com/best-time-planting-trees/.

———. "Planting Trees the Right Way." Garden Fundamentals (website). Accessed May 12, 2021. gardenfundamentals.com/planting-trees-right-way/.

Perry, Leonard. "Effective Deer Fences." University of Vermont, Department of Plant and Soil Sciences, The Green Mountain Gardener blog. Accessed May 11, 2021. pss.uvm.edu/ppp/articles/deerfences.html.

Pevach (website). "Your Guide to Hardy, Fast Growing Trees in Alberta and Saskatchewan." January 23, 2019. pevachcorp.com/tree-tips/your-guide-to-hardy-fast -growing-trees-in-alberta-and-saskatchewan.

Phys.org (website). "Northern Gardening Tips: When Fruit Trees Don't Bear Fruit, What's the Problem?" May 28, 2007. phys.org/news/2007-05-northern-gardening-fruit -trees-dont.html.

Planet Natural Research Center (website). "Leaf Spot." Accessed May 11, 2021. planetnatural.com/pest-problem-solver/plant-disease/bacterial-leaf-spot/.

Reich, Lee. "Tree Planting 101 (Hint: It's Not What You've Heard)." Old House Online (website). oldhouseonline.com/gardens-and-exteriors/tree-planting-101-hint-youve -heard/.

Rosenthal, Ed. *Protect Your Garden: Eco-Friendly Solutions for Healthy Plants.* San Francisco, CA: Quick American Archives, 2013.

Ruzycki, Brenda. "Drought-Tolerant Plants." *Edmonton Sun.* April 29, 2012. edmontonsun.com/2012/04/28/drought–tolerant-plants.

Sadof, Clifford S. "Landscape and Ornamentals: Scale Insects on Shade Trees and Shrubs." Purdue University Extension, Entomology. January 2017. extension.entm .purdue.edu/publications/E-29/E-29.html.

Scheufele, Susan B., Ross Norton, and Rick Harper. "Protecting Evergreens in the Winter Q&A." University of Massachusetts Amherst, Center for Agriculture, Food, and the Environment. January 2015. ag.umass.edu/landscape/fact-sheets/protecting -evergreens-in-winter-qa.

Schill, Jerry. "Why Are My Trees and Shrubs Not Leafing Out?" Schill Grounds Management (website). June 5, 2017. schilllandscaping.com/blog/why-are-my-trees -and-shrubs-not-leafing-out.

Science Learning Hub (website). "What Is a Tree?" July 3, 2018. sciencelearn .org.nz/resources/2636-what-is-a-tree#:~:text=Trees%20are%20all%20plants%20 and,include%20trees%20are%20vascular%20plants.

Sellmer, Jim, J. Robert Nuss, and Scott Guiser. "Trees, Shrubs, and Ground Covers Tolerant of Wet Sites." Penn State Extension. October 22, 2007. extension.psu .edu/trees-shrubs-and-groundcovers-tolerant-of-wet-sites.

SFGate (website). "What Type of Whitewash to Put on Fruit Trees?" October 23, 2020. homeguides.sfgate.com/type-whitewash-put-fruit-trees-61693.html.

———. "Will a Squirrel Stripping the Bark off My Tree Kill the Tree?" May 24, 2021. homeguides.sfgate.com/squirrel-stripping-bark-off-tree-kill-tree-92677.html.

Sherrill, Ursula, and Margaret C. Brittingham. "Landscaping for Wildlife: Trees, Shrubs, and Vines." Last updated January 1, 2001. Penn State Extension. extension.psu .edu/landscaping-for-wildlife-trees-shrubs-and-vines.

Sherwood's Forests (website). "Buying Trees: Big Trees Lead to a Skinny Wallet." Accessed May 8, 2021. sherwoods-forests.com/Ideas/Buying_Trees.html.

———. "Fall Colour: You Can Have Something Besides Yellow." Accessed May 12, 2021. sherwoods-forests.com/Ideas/Fall_Colour.html.

———. "Hedges: What Are They Good For?" Accessed May 12, 2021. sherwoods -forests.com/Ideas/Hedges.html.

Skinner, Hugh, and Sara Williams. *Best Trees and Shrubs for the Prairies.* Calgary: Fifth House Publishers, 2004.

Smith, Ron. "Basic Guidelines for Pruning Trees and Shrubs." North Dakota State University. Last updated April 2015. ag.ndsu.edu/publications/lawns-gardens-trees /basic-guidelines-for-pruning-trees-and-shrubs.

Spengler, Teo. "Tree Leaves Didn't Drop in Winter: Reasons Why Leaves Did Not Fall Off a Tree." Gardening Know How (website). Last updated September 1, 2020. gardeningknowhow.com/ornamental/trees/tgen/why-leaves-did-not-fall-off-tree.htm.

Sproule, Rob. "Your Pruning Calendar." Salisbury Greenhouse (website). Accessed May 13, 2021. salisburygreenhouse.com/your-pruning-calendar/.

Squirrel Enthusiast (website). "Why Do Squirrels Eat Bark and What You Can Do about It." Accessed May 12, 2021. squirrelenthusiast.com/why-do-squirrels-eat-bark/.

Stelzer, Hank. "First Aid for Storm-Damaged Trees." University of Missouri Extension. May 2017. extension.missouri.edu/publications/g6867.

Sunstar Nurseries (website). "Deciduous Trees." Accessed May 12, 2021. sunstarnurseries.com/deciduous-trees.html.

———. "Evergreens." Accessed May 12, 2021. sunstarnurseries.com/evergreens.html.

Tree Canada (website). "Northern Hackberry (*Celtis occidentalis*)." Accessed May 12, 2021. treecanada.ca/resources/trees-of-canada/northern-hackberry-celtis-occidentalis/.

———. "Trees of Canada." Accessed May 12, 2021. treecanada.ca/resources/trees-of -canada/.

Tree Ottawa (website). "Planting a Caliper Tree." Accessed May 10, 2021. treeottawa .wordpress.com/plant/how-to-plant-a-tree/caliper/.

Trees.com (website). "Cedar Mulch in the Garden—Uses, Pros and Cons, and Problems." Last updated March 4, 2020. trees.com/gardening-and-landscaping/cedar-mulch.

———. "11 Best Evergreen Ground Cover Plants That Make Your Garden Look Greener and Better." Last updated July 12, 2019. trees.com/ground-cover-plants /evergreen-ground-cover-plants.

Trees Winnipeg (website). "Dutch Elm Disease." Accessed May 15, 2021. treeswinnipeg.org/our-urban-forest/urban-forest-threats/dutch-elm -disease#:~:text=Elm%20bark%20beetles%20are%20highly,at%20any%20time%20 of%20year.

Tree Time (website). "Common Hackberry vs. Prairie Sky Poplar." Accessed May 12, 2021. treetime.ca/compare.php?pcids=59-287.

———. "Fall Colour Plants." Accessed May 12, 2021. treetime.ca/products .php?tagid=28.

———. "What Are the Best Fast Growing Trees in Alberta?" Accessed May 12, 2021. treetime.ca/fast-growing-trees-in-alberta.php.

Tree Weaver (website). "Epicormic Sprouts and Their Role in the Health of the Tree." Accessed May 15, 2021. treeweaverarborist.com/epicormic-sprouts-and-their-role-in-the -health-of-the-tree/.

University of Illinois Extension. "Decline and Dieback of Trees and Shrubs." April 1996. ipm.illinois.edu/diseases/series600/rpd641/.

University of Manitoba, Faculty of Agriculture and Food Sciences. "Pruning Deciduous Ornamentals." Accessed May 13, 2021. umanitoba.ca/faculties/afs/hort_inquiries/2234 .html.

University of Minnesota Extension. "Watering Established Trees and Shrubs." 2018. extension.umn.edu/planting-and-growing-guides/watering-established-trees-and -shrubs#when-to-water-trees-and-shrubs-1261760.

Valk, Sean. "Downy Mildew vs. Powdery Mildew." Greenhouse Canada (website). August 14, 2008. greenhousecanada.com/downy-mildew-vs-powdery-mildew-1594/.

Virginia Cooperative Extension. "A Guide to Successful Pruning: Pruning Deciduous Trees." Last updated December 2009. jccwmg.org/PDF/PruningHandbook3.2009.pdf.

Walliser, Jessica. "Dwarf Evergreen Trees: 15 Exceptional Choices for the Yard and Garden." Savvy Gardening (website). Accessed May 12, 2021. savvygardening.com /dwarf-evergreen-trees/.

Weber, Lillian M., Graeme Pierce Berlyn, and Thomas H. Everett. "Tree." Britannica (website). July 8, 2007. britannica.com/plant/tree/Popular-classifications.

Williams, Sara. *Creating the Prairie Xeriscape*. Regina: Coteau Books, 2013.

Williamson, Don. *Tree and Shrub Gardening for Alberta*. Tukwila, WA: Lone Pine Publishing, 2009.

Wood, Tim. "No More Weeding or Mulching: Ground Covering Shrubs." The Plant Hunter (website). Accessed May 12, 2021. plant-quest.blogspot.com/2010/09/ground -covering-shrubs.html.

Zuzek, Kathy. "Watering Newly Planted Trees and Shrubs." University of Minnesota Extension. 2018. extension.umn.edu/planting-and-growing-guides/watering-newly -planted-trees-and-shrubs.

Index

Page numbers in italics refer to photographs.

trunk, 7, 9, 12, 31, 34, 37–38, 61, 70–71, 104

turfgrass. *See* lawn

U

union, graft, 17

urine, dog, 64

utility lines, 24

V

vegetable, 94

viburnum, 39, 108, 110, 117, 122, 125, 129

vole, 82, 103

W

walking stick, Harry Lauder's, 113

wasps, 91

    parasitoid, 88

water, 20, 29–30, 37, 40, 64, 66, 68, 76, 121, 123

    loss, 37

    movement of, 7, 9, 51, 61, 95, 97

    percolation, 36

watering, 7, 23, 37–38, 48, 64, 73, 85, 90, 100

    winter freeze-up, 40, *40*

water sprouts, 71, *71*

weather, 8, 37, 64, 66, 73, 77, 93

weeding, 41, 58

weigela, 45, 108, 118

well, tree, 27, *27*–28

    dry, 28

whitewash, 51

willow, 69, 113, 117, 122–23, 126

wind, 31, 53, 55, 79, 119, 123, 127

winter, *67*, 95

    desiccation, *65*

    dormancy, 70

    early onset, 123

    heat, unseasonable, 64

    root growth, 29

    survival, 40

    temperatures, extreme, 58, 66, 119, 127

    wildlife damage, 102–03

wintercreeper euonymus, 118

winterkill, 66–67

woadwaxen. *See* lydia broom

woodlice. *See* sowbugs

woodpeckers, 104

woody plants, 7, 26, 29, 34, 40, 48, 66

    age, 58, 66, 74

    ball-and-burlapped, 20, *21*

    bare-root. *See* bare-root plants

    compact, 114–15

    container-grown, 15, 22–23, 37, 61

    for damp sites, 122

    drought tolerant, 121

    fast-growing, 123

    hardwood, 123

    importance to humans, 7

    large shade, 126

    ornamental. *See* flowering trees and shrubs

    part shade, 124–25

    poisonous, 125

    science of, 9

    shelterbelt, 127–28, *128*

    size, 12

    small-space selections, 17

    softwood, 123

    wildlife- and bird-friendly, 7, 129

wildlife, 61, 70, 82, 118, 129

woody tissue, secondary, 9

wrap, tree, 51

X

xylem, 9, 62, 64

Y

yew, 117, *124*, 125

© Steve Melrose

156

About the Authors

SHERYL NORMANDEAU was born and raised in the Peace Country region of northern Alberta and has made Calgary her home since 1994. A writer and master gardener, Sheryl holds a bachelor's degree in English, as well as a Prairie Horticulture Certificate and an Urban Sustainable Agriculture Certificate. Since 2013, she has served as the online Ask an Expert for the Calgary Horticultural Society. She works at the Calgary Public Library—besides gardening, books of all kinds are her grand passion! She is a small-space gardener (on a tiny balcony and in a plot in a nearby community garden) and she is most enthusiastic about growing veggies. In addition to the Guides for the Prairie Gardener series, Sheryl is the author of the cookbook *The Little Prairie Book of Berries: Recipes for Saskatoons, Sea Buckthorn, Haskap Berries and More*. She lives with her husband, Rob, and their rescue cat Smudge. Find Sheryl at Flowery Prose (floweryprose .com) and on Facebook (@FloweryProse), Twitter (@Flowery_Prose), and Instagram (flowery_prose).

JANET MELROSE was born in Trinidad, West Indies, and immigrated to Canada in 1964. She has lived in Calgary since 1969. She is a master gardener and the creator and owner of the successful horticulture business Calgary's Cottage Gardener, which specializes in garden education and consultation, horticultural therapy, and advocating for sustainable local food systems. She holds bachelor's degrees in sociology and history, a Prairie Horticulture Certificate, and a Horticultural Therapy Certificate. Janet is a lifelong gardener, coming from a heritage of English gardening. She has a large garden at home in the suburbs of Calgary that can only be described as a typical cottage garden. She cares for eight other gardens throughout Calgary through her work as a horticultural therapist, as well as a bed at the Inglewood Community Garden. She is married to Steve and has two children, Jennifer and David. Three cats, Patrick, Theo, and Mia, currently own their home and patrol against the deer, hares, squirrels, skunk, mice, insects, and assorted birds that believe the garden is theirs, too! Connect with Janet on Facebook (@Calgarys-Cottage-Gardener), Twitter (@CalCottageGrdnr), and Instagram (CalgarysCottageGardener).

About the Series

It looks like you've discovered the Guides for the Prairie Gardener! This budding series puts the combined knowledge of two lifelong prairie gardeners at your grubby fingertips. Whether you've just cleared a few square feet for your first bed of veggies or are a seasoned green thumb stumped by that one cultivar you can't seem to master, we think you'll find Janet and Sheryl the ideal teachers. Find answers on seeds, soil, trees, flowers, weather, climate, pests, pots, and quite a few more topics. These slim but mighty volumes, handsomely designed, make great companions at the height of summer in the garden trenches and during cold winter days planning the next season. With regional expertise, elegance, and a sense of humour, Janet and Sheryl take your questions and turn them into prairie gardening inspiration. For more information, and for other titles in the series, visit touchwoodeditions.com/guidesprairiegardener.